EXCERPTING AMERICAN HISTORY FROM 1877 TO 2001

Primary Sources and Commentary

First Edition

Written and edited by
J. Edward Lee, Ph.D.

Winthrop University

SAN DIEGO

Bassim Hamadeh, CEO and Publisher
Peaches diPierro, DevelopmentalEditor
Alisa Munoz, Project Editor
Jeanine Rees, Production Editor
Jess Estrella, Senior Graphic Designer
Greg Isales, Licensing Coordinator
Natalie Piccotti, Director of Marketing
Kassie Graves, Vice President of Editorial
Jamie Giganti, Director of Academic Publishing

Copyright © 2022 by Cognella, Inc. All rights reserved. No part of this publication may be reprinted, reproduced, transmitted, or utilized in any form or by any electronic, mechanical, or other means, now known or hereafter invented, including photocopying, microfilming, and recording, or in any information retrieval system without the written permission of Cognella, Inc. For inquiries regarding permissions, translations, foreign rights, audio rights, and any other forms of reproduction, please contact the Cognella Licensing Department at rights@cognella.com.

Trademark Notice: Product or corporate names may be trademarks or registered trademarks and are used only for identification and explanation without intent to infringe.

Cover image copyright © 2013 Depositphotos/pavila1.
Cover image copyright © 2008 iStockphoto LP/NSA Digital Archive.
Cover image copyright © 2018 iStockphoto LP/Nastasic.
Cover image copyright © 2019 iStockphoto LP/Keith Lance.
Cover image copyright © 2020 iStockphoto LP/duncan1890.

Printed in the United States of America.

EXCERPTING AMERICAN HISTORY
FROM 1877 TO 2001

For my grandchildren, Madeline Walen and Connor Walen.

Brief Contents

Acknowledgments   xiii
Introduction   xv

Chapter 1   Bold Entrepreneurs   1

Chapter 2   The Arena   7

Chapter 3   Looseness   14

Chapter 4   The Greatest Generation   20

Chapter 5   Containment   29

Chapter 6   Barriers   35

Chapter 7   New Frontiers   41

Chapter 8   Roller Coaster   48

Chapter 9   Malaise   53

Chapter 10   Morning   60

Conclusion: Walls and Towers   67
Document Sources   69
About the Author   71

Detailed Contents

Acknowledgments   xiii
Introduction   xv

CHAPTER 1

Bold Entrepreneurs   1
Document 1.1. Constitution of the Knights of Labor   3
   Thinking Historically   4
Document 1.2. *Triumphant Democracy*   4
   Thinking Historically   5
Document 1.3. *How the Other Half Lives*   5
   Thinking Historically   5
Document 1.4. Map of the United States, 1900   6
   Thinking Historically   6

CHAPTER 2

The Arena   7
Document 2.1. Beveridge's Address to Congress   10
   Thinking Historically   11
Document 2.2. "The Man in the Arena"   11
   Thinking Historically   11
Document 2.3. Woodrow Wilson's Declaration of War   12
   Thinking Historically   12
Document 2.4. Paris Peace Conference Map, 1919   12
   Thinking Historically   13

CHAPTER 3

Looseness   14
Document 3.1. Warren G. Harding's Inaugural Address   16
   Thinking Historically   16
Document 3.2. The Klan's Fight for Americanism   17
   Thinking Historically   17
Document 3.3. *The Great Gatsby*   17
   Thinking Historically   18
Document 3.4. Henry Ford's Philosophy   18
   Thinking Historically   19

CHAPTER 4

The Greatest Generation   20

Document 4.1. *Hard Times*   24
    Thinking Historically   25
Document 4.2. Franklin D. Roosevelt's Inaugural Address   25
    Thinking Historically   25
Document 4.3. Roosevelt's "Quarantine" Speech   26
    Thinking Historically   26
Document 4.4. Nesei Internment   26
    Thinking Historically   27
Document 4.5. Maps of Europe and Asia, World War II   27
    Thinking Historically   28

CHAPTER 5

Containment   29

Document 5.1. Winston Churchill's "Iron Curtain" Speech, 1946   31
    Thinking Historically   31
Document 5.2. Senator McCarthy's Radio Address, 1950   32
    Thinking Historically   32
Document 5.3. "Declaration of Conscience"   32
    Thinking Historically   33
Document 5.4. Truman Fires General MacArthur   33
    Thinking Historically   33
Document 5.5. Map of the Cold War   34
    Thinking Historically   34

CHAPTER 6

Barriers   35

Document 6.1. *Brown v. Board of Education*   37
    Thinking Historically   38
Document 6.2. Dwight D. Eisenhower's Radio Address, 1957   38
    Thinking Historically   38
Document 6.3. The Eisenhower Doctrine   39
    Thinking Historically   39
Document 6.4. Civil Rights Protests in 1960   39
    Thinking Historically   40
Document 6.5. Eisenhower's Farewell Address   40
    Thinking Historically   40

CHAPTER 7

New Frontiers   41

Document 7.1. John F. Kennedy's Inaugural Address   44
  Thinking Historically   44
Document 7.2. JFK's TV Address During the Cuban Missile Crisis   45
  Thinking Historically   45
Document 7.3. Adlai Stevenson's UN Speech   45
  Thinking Historically   46
Document 7.4. Lyndon B. Johnson's War on Poverty   46
  Thinking Historically   46
Document 7.5. Fannie Lou Hamer's Democratic Convention Speech, 1964   47
  Thinking Historically   47

CHAPTER 8

Roller Coaster   48

Document 8.1. The Gulf of Tonkin Incident   50
  Thinking Historically   50
Document 8.2. Johnson's Comments on the Gulf of Tonkin Resolution   51
  Thinking Historically   51
Document 8.3. Johnson's Defense of the Vietnam War   52
  Thinking Historically   52

CHAPTER 9

Malaise   53

Document 9.1. Neil Armstrong Walks on the Moon   56
  Thinking Historically   56
Document 9.2. Richard Nixon's Incursion Announcement   56
  Thinking Historically   57
Document 9.3. Nixon Announces "Peace With Honor" in Vietnam   57
  Thinking Historically   58
Document 9.4. Nixon's White House Tapes   58
  Thinking Historically   58
Document 9.5. Jimmy Carter's Call for Energy Conservation   59
  Thinking Historically   59

CHAPTER 10

Morning   60

Document 10.1. Ronald Reagan's Economic Philosophy   62
  Thinking Historically   62

Document 10.2. Reagan's Optimism on Democracy   63
   Thinking Historically   63
Document 10.3. Brzezinski's Support for DSI   63
   Thinking Historically   64
Document 10.4. The Boland Amendment   64
   Thinking Historically   64
Document 10.5. The End of the Cold War   65
   Thinking Historically   65
Document 10.6. George W. Bush's 9/11 Address   65
   Thinking Historically   66

Conclusion: Walls and Towers   67
Document Sources   69
About the Author   71

Acknowledgments

Throughout my 36-six years in the university classroom, I have been fortunate to have inspiring mentors who shared their advice and wisdom. While pursuing my master's degree at Winthrop University, history professors Thomas Morgan, Ross Webb, and James Cassada helped me refine my research and writing skills. My graduate assistantship in the university archives, under the directorship of Professor Ron Chepesiuk, helped me gain insight into the treasures stored in that quiet place.

While earning my doctorate at the University of South Carolina, I served as president of the Graduate Students Association. I attended faculty meetings and learned something about academia. Professors George Rogers, Lacy Ford, John Duffy, and Ed Cox helped me develop my teaching style. Early in my career, these scholars hired me to teach adult learners, a constituency that is crucial to higher education.

I have been able to learn from the very best scholars at Winthrop University, the University of South Carolina, and the University of North Carolina at Charlotte. At the latter institution, I became friends with Professor David Goldfield, who I watched begin each day early. I continue that commendable work habit. At Winthrop University, I observed my retired colleague, Professor Jason Silverman, prove that students could be entertained as well as intellectually stimulated.

Students, past and present, are important in my life. I enjoy their energy, questions, and spirit. The total is more than 10,000, and I eagerly look forward to teaching those yet to sit in my classrooms.

Always, I acknowledge my family: wife Ann-Franklin Hardy Lee, daughter Elizabeth Ann Walen, son-in-law Corey Walen, parents Tyre Douglas Lee and Ola Bankhead Lee, and my grandchildren, to whom this volume is dedicated. Scholars and kin have made me who I have become. I thank them all!

J. Edward Lee, PhD
York, South Carolina

Introduction

Publisher Henry Luce, the son of a missionary, wrote in *Life* magazine that the twentieth century was "the American Century." Luce was describing the dark time of 1941. Demons were on the loose, pillaging Europe and Asia. He reminded us that our nation possessed "magnificent purposes." He urged us, the citadel of freedom, to forsake isolationism and prepare for Adolph Hitler, Benito Mussolini, and the Japanese military. He considered that "our mission." We were to lead the world. It was expected.

This work begins before the dawn of "the American Century." In 1877, the 12 years of the Reconstruction Era had ended in failure. Many racist attitudes had not been erased; the plight of former slaves had wearied national leaders who wished to escape memories of the Civil War; the United States moved into what writer Mark Twain labeled "the Gilded Age." There would be no room for freedmen and freedwomen; our interests lay elsewhere in 1877.

From 1877 until 1901, the captains of industry and their inventor friends dominated a nation focused on profit and economic growth for some. Others, new immigrants, farmers, African Americans, women, for instance, were left out of prosperity—excluded. It would be the fabulously wealthy bold entrepreneurs with names like Rockefeller, Carnegie, and Morgan who directed our country until the beginning of Luce's "American Century." The Gilded Age's presidents, Hayes, Garfield, Arthur, Cleveland, Harrison, and McKinley stood in the shadows of these captains of industry.

For two decades, from 1901 through 1920, progress manifest itself in Theodore Roosevelt's Square Deal, William Howard Taft's trustbusting, and Woodrow Wilson's New Freedom. These progressive presidents reformed and regulated our economy and society, but, still, not all Americans benefited, as crusading journalists, "muckrakers," revealed in numerous publications.

As this volume makes clear, we are, indeed, a "magnificent" nation. Unfortunately, we often exclude people from our progress. Remember: we excluded Chinese immigrants; we slowly granted suffrage to women; we segregated the races; we abandoned farmers. Barriers were established, and we must examine their causes. Have these obstacles been removed in the twenty-first century?

We have stepped forward, as Henry Luce wished, to lead in times of global crisis: the Great War and the Second World War. Courage and sacrifice, by all races, genders, and military ranks, have been displayed on battlefields around the globe.

This anthology explores the Jazz Age and Harlem Renaissance, a burst of artistic creativity. The 1920s were loose years, flappers and their dates dancing the nights away. The politics and economic policies were even looser. We will consider the costs of this looseness during the Great Depression of 1929 through 1941, a decade-long international hangover.

The Greatest Generation stepped forward to fight the ravages of the Great Depression, and President Franklin D. Roosevelt's New Deal demonstrated the best of the resilient American spirit in war and peace.

During the American Century, we became immersed in global crusades, a Cold War between us and our allies and the Soviet Union and its allies. Wars in Korea and Vietnam, standing at the brink in Berlin and the Middle East, rebuilding ravaged Europe and Japan, and watching uneasily as communism triumphed in Eastern Europe and China are important landmarks to our understanding of the period under review in this book. Certainly, we occasionally brushed up against yet another world war. Consider the Cuban Missile Crisis of 1962.

But it was a time of cultural and scientific exploration. Television, music, movies, literature, the arts, sports, science, technology, and outer space were essential parts of what President John F. Kennedy called the New Frontier. Compassion for the poor, advances in civil and gender rights, and concern for the environment were hallmarks of this era. By 1969, Americans had set foot on the moon, one small step but a giant leap for our nation.

Economic challenges in the 1970s, such as skyrocketing oil prices, a disgraced president, and an economic malaise, created challenges as we celebrated our bicentennial in 1976. Three years later, fifty-two Americans were held hostage for 444 days in the Middle East. One presidency was wrecked by the ordeal, and another full of optimism and bravado took its place. The Cold War came to an end as communism collapsed upon itself in 1989. Were we now the only superpower?

In this anthology, we will step backward in time, commencing with the thud that ended the failure of Reconstruction in 1877 and proceed 124 years until we reach the terrorist attacks of 2001. Also, as we conclude our study, we will ponder where we as a nation find ourselves in the community of nations in the twenty-first century. Will this, too, be the American Century?

These United States: Themes, Cycles, and Echoes

As students of history, we ask questions about the past, and we seek answers by sorting through the raw materials, such as government documents, newspaper accounts, manuscripts, letters, diaries, and speeches. These are history's primary sources. From them, we analyze the evidence, data, and information and form judgments about our past. While history does not really repeat itself, we can hear the echoes of the voices of people who lived years ago. Themes and cycles emerge.

Historians weigh this evidence and inquire about its significance. We want to understand those people who came before us. Who were they? When and where did they live?

What were their conditions? How did the environment affect them? What challenges did they face? What were their eras like? Who were their families and friends? Did they succeed or fail in life? Did they achieve their goals? How did they interact with others? Did they have power? Are we a violent people? Are our intentions noble? These are some of history's questions.

This anthology allows us to answer these questions by sharply focusing on the period of 1877 through 2001. The author has asked these questions for 36 years of university classroom experience. He has identified themes that flow through US history: the good and bad use of power, conflict, and consensus, equality, human rights and dignity, restlessness, wealth distribution, independence, security, ingenuity, and achievement. Our nation's history is full of such themes, and we can hear echoes of the past by examining and pondering them.

Each chapter of this book begins with an introductory essay prepared by me. It is the product of my decades of scholarship and the questions that I have asked over the years. Fifty documents have been carefully selected and excerpted. They come from the raw material that I mentioned. I introduce these documents, five of which are maps, and place them in historical context. After each document, I have created an exercise called "Thinking Historically," consisting of five questions. Mull over these questions, prepare your answers, speak with your instructor and classmates. Research them. Use these questions as springboards for additional research. Dig deeply. We decide what the answers to "Thinking Historically" might be. I encourage you to reassess your opinions when needed. We take slivers of the past and let them speak to us.

As we start our review of the period of 1877 through 2001, I have chosen three documents that will illustrate the anthology's approach. Listen for the echoes of our country's past, explore its cycles, and identify themes that define America.

Document 0.1. The New Colossus

Coming to America in search of a better life has been a theme of our history since those first people walked across Beringia, the frozen land bridge connecting Asia and North America, 30,000 years ago. Immigration has populated the continent. Old immigrants like the British and French interacted with the indigenous population for centuries, trading and competing for natural resources in this paradise. The Dutch, Irish, Germans, and people in bondage arrived. In the late nineteenth century, the strong relationship between Americans and France, stretching back to the latter nation's invaluable assistance in our struggle for independence from our mother country of Great Britain in the American Revolution resulted in a gift: the Statue of Liberty in New York City on Ellis Island, which would welcome new immigrants, people from Poland, Russia, Greece, Italy, and other lands, who brought their hopes and dreams and little else. Their names were different, as were their religions, but they came here for a better life than they had in the Old World. Funds were raised for a pedestal for the massive statue. Finally, in 1883, Emma Lazarus, a passionate member of a prominent Jewish family, spelled out the promise of America in words at the statue's base. The following excerpt is her poetry, which is emblazoned on the Statue of Liberty, facing toward the ocean in the city's harbor, the first glimpse of their new home that those immigrants saw as they came ashore.

> "Keep, ancient lands, your storied pomp!" cries she with silent lips. "Give me your tired, your poor, your huddled masses yearning to breathe free, the wretched refuse of your tempest-tost to me, I lift my lamp beside the golden door."

Thinking Historically

1. Differentiate between the challenges awaiting the new immigrants and those who had come earlier.
2. Why did the captains of industry welcome the new immigrants?
3. How would their languages and religions hamper the assimilation of the new immigrants?
4. What does "storied pomp" of the Old World mean?
5. Why were America's cities natural destination points for the new immigrants?

Document 0.2. *The Souls of Black Folk*

When African American Booker T. Washington, who had close ties to the captains of industry, was invited in 1895 to address the Cotton States Exposition in the New South city of Atlanta, Georgia, some expected him to speak out against segregation, racism, and the lynching of Black Americans. In the Gilded Age, Washington solicited financial support from the industrialists for segregated trade schools. In Atlanta, he mildly avoided confronting his powerful financial backers and spoke of accommodation instead of confrontation. He spoke of humans being one hand but separate fingers. He meekly avoided the brutal topic of lynching. The criticism from militant critics was harsh. The following is Dr. W.E.B. Du Bois's response to Washington's remarks, which Du Bois, the first African American to earn a Harvard doctorate, considered a weak response to the problems faced by African Americans in the Gilded Age.

> Mr. Washington represents in Negro thought the old attitude of adjustment and submission; but adjustment at such a peculiar time as to make his programme unique. This is an age of unusual economic development, and Mr. Washington's programme naturally takes an economic cast, becoming a gospel of Work and Money to such an extent as apparently almost completely to overshadow the higher aims of life. ... Mr. Washington distinctly asks that black people give up, at least for

the present, three things—First, political power, Second, insistence on civil rights, Third, higher education of Negro youth,—and concentrate their energies on industrial education, the accumulation of wealth, and the conciliation of the South.

Thinking Historically

1. What, exactly, is Dr. Du Bois's criticism of Mr. Washington, and is it justified?
2. Why would Booker T. Washington be hesitant in 1895 to publicly denounce the era's racism?
3. What audience was Washington trying to influence with his Atlanta remarks?
4. Why was Washington's speech sometimes referred to as the "Atlanta Compromise"?
5. Does this disagreement between Du Bois and Washington indicate a split in the civil rights movement of the Gilded Age?

Document 0.3. *Roe v. Wade*

The issue of abortion continues to be debated in present-day America. In the early 1970s, this procedure was legal in some states but forbidden elsewhere. In 1973, a pregnant Texas single mother, identified publicly as "Jane Roe," became, with the support of various organizations such as the National Organization of Women, the plaintiff in a suit against the state of Texas over its pro-life stance. To "Roe" and her allies, the decision to abort a fetus was a private choice that a pregnant woman with the advice of her physician should have as an option. In its *Roe v. Wade* ruling, the all-male US Supreme Court issued a landmark decision, excerpted next, which supported a pregnant women's due process and privacy rights, allowing abortions within the first trimester of pregnancy. The court examined issues of choice, "viability" of human life concerning fetus and health of the mother, and the role played by expectant mothers.

(a) For the stage prior to approximately the end of the first trimester, the abortion decision and its effectuation must be left to the medical judgment of the pregnant woman's physician.

(b) For the stage subsequent to approximately the end of the first trimester, the State, in promoting its interest in the health of the mother, may, if it chooses, regulate the abortion procedure in ways that are reasonably related to maternal health.

(c) For the stage subsequent to viability the State, in promoting its interest in the potentiality of human life, may, if it chooses, regulate, and even proscribe, abortion except where it is necessary, in appropriate medical judgment, for the preservation of the life of or health of the mother.

Thinking Historically

1. How did *Roe v. Wade* ignite a national debate between pro-life and pro-choice citizens?
2. Was this decision hampered by the fact that nine male justices considered the case?
3. What are your thoughts about fetus "viability" and the court's stance that the first trimester should normally be used as the time line for abortions?
4. Were there economic factors in Texas in the early 1970s that prevented a woman like "Jane Roe" from traveling to New York for an abortion?
5. How did "privacy" issues affect this landmark ruling?

BOLD ENTREPRENEURS

The American Civil War cost 750,000 lives. The southern states were devastated by the conflict, with their cotton economy wrecked by Union troops and slaves seeking freedom as the war progressed. For 12 years, 1865 through 1877, the nation tried to rebuild itself, assist the freedmen and freedwomen, and change southern racist attitudes toward African Americans. This period, the Reconstruction Era, was a disappointing failure. The South's infrastructure was slow to recover after the Civil War, and occupying northern troops had their hands full with organizations such as the Ku Klux Klan, which terrorized the ex-slaves and tried to intimidate them to keep them from voting, even though the Fifteenth Amendment to the Constitution, ratified in 1870, gave African American males the right to cast ballots. Howard University philosophy professor Alain Locke called it the "nadir of the Negro," a low point in civil rights. A disputed presidential election in 1876 between Ohio's Republican governor Rutherford B. Hayes and New York's Democratic governor Samuel J. Tilden was settled by a questionable agreement, which gave victory to Hayes but withdrew the remaining Union troops from the South as part of the deal. The country, in 1877, seemed weary of Reconstruction and its cost. Hayes focused on economic development instead of racial equality. The president would be overshadowed by captains of industry, bold entrepreneurs, and inventors who were ready to abandon African Americans and concentrate on our growing economy, accumulating huge fortunes.

Writer Mark Twain called the period 1877 through 1901 "the Gilded Age." It was a time when new immigrants arrived on our shores (see Document 0.1), the rich became richer, and "the other half," as reformer Jacob Riis called them (see Document 1.3), were ignored. Groups such as these immigrants who reformer Jane Addams tried to assist with her Hull House in Chicago, farmers, remaining Native Americans, women, and African Americans were deemed not important to the future of America. The Supreme Court in 1896 drew a color line between the races in its *Plessy v. Ferguson* ruling. The bold entrepreneurs and their allies dominated the country at the expense of these citizens. Power and attention had dramatically shifted to corporate board rooms. Economically, we raced along during the Gilded Age, but many people were excluded from opportunities to advance. It was an era when the strong and well-connected ruled America; they prospered and survived at the expense of many others who were deemed disposable.

Even before the Gilded Age commenced, the captains of industry mobilized. One of the earliest was Cornelius Vanderbilt of New York, known as "the Commodore." His wealth was based on shipping and railroads, the New York Central and the Harlem. Early, he transformed steamships into sleek vessels for trade. In the Civil War, "the Commodore" offered some of his vessels to the Union navy. President Abraham Lincoln rejected the offer because he valued the commercial vitality of Vanderbilt's empire. In 1869, this entrepreneur laid the groundwork for Grand Central Depot, which evolved into Grand Central Station. The Vanderbilt family constructed the Biltmore House near Asheville, North Carolina, the largest private residence in America, even though the Vanderbilts considered it "a hunting lodge." It was a lavish statement of the wealth that "the Commodore" had accumulated through his economic ventures.

One of the wealthiest people in America during the Gilded Age was banking magnate J. Pierpont Morgan, whose financial empire, "the House of Morgan," controlled the nation's banks beginning in 1871. His firm grasp on banking was acknowledged by everyone, even President Grover Cleveland who had to negotiate with Morgan in 1893 for an infusion of badly needed gold into the national treasury. Morgan's power influenced the media, which tried to publish flattering photographs of the banker. In the Progressive Era (see Chapter 2), Morgan would joust with President Theodore Roosevelt over the monopolistic "House of Morgan."

John D. Rockefeller built his fortune supplying Union troops during the Civil War, but it was his effort in the 1870s to see that the future of America would require oil that dramatically increased his wealth. Rockefeller began Standard Oil and drove competitors out of business if they refused to sell their smaller oil companies to him. He understood the importance of oil and the need to transport it quickly on the network of railroads springing up across America. Like Vanderbilt, he showed off his power in estates and lectured school children about the importance of money well into his ninth decade. His brand became known in real estate, Rockefeller Center, and universities as he remained active even when the Progressives insisted on oil-producing competition.

Scottish immigrant Alexander Graham Bell, like Rockefeller, was a visionary. In 1876, his company's telephone revolutionized communication, replacing the telegraph. By 1900, more Americans had telephones in their homes than indoor bathrooms. Similarly, Thomas A. Edison's electric light bulb and the formation in 1878 of Edison Electric Light Company (with the backing of the House of Morgan) changed the way Americans lived. By 1901, President William McKinley would light up the fairgrounds in Buffalo, New York, turning darkness into light for the people watching him flip a switch during the World's Fair.

Lancaster, Pennsylvania, entrepreneur Frank Woolworth created a small "dime store" empire, which stretched from Lancaster across the country beginning in 1879. The business model was simple: once people entered his store for one item, within a few minutes they purchased multiple things from soap to nails. Safeguarding business profits, Ohio's John H. Patterson took his "thief catcher" in 1884 and his 13 employees at National Manufacturing Company and sold cash registers across the land. Recording this economic development was Rochester, New York's George Eastman, who produced affordable cameras, a "Kodak" he called it. These instruments had the film securely locked inside. Enamored customers purchased the Kodak, took the photographs, and mailed the camera back to Eastman, whose technicians developed the film and mailed a new camera and the memories back to customers.

Throughout the Gilded Age, these bold entrepreneurs gained prominence, wealth, and power. Typical was Scottish immigrant Andrew Carnegie who founded in 1892 the Carnegie Steel Company, supplying steel for a land that was steadily becoming more urban. He spoke of "the Gospel of Wealth" (see Document 1.2). With the backing of J. P. Morgan, United States Steel became America's first billion-dollar corporation, making sure that industrial laborers, who worked in dangerous and unhealthy environments, did not interfere with economic development and profits for the captains of industry. These laborers were organizing in the Gilded Age, advocating for safer conditions and better pay, as well as relief from grueling 12-hour workdays. In 1886, there had been a clash between the Knights of Labor and management (who had police support) in the streets of Chicago during the Haymarket Square Riot (see Document 1.1).

By the end of the Gilded Age, the remaining Native Americans lamented what had happened to the indigenous people, who had lost their land and were forced to live on poorly funded reservations with problems such as alcoholism and inadequate educational opportunities. Farmers, sensing the tilt toward cities and banks, rebelled in 1896 as Nebraska's William Jennings Bryan called for "free silver," which would lessen the clout of the gold controlled by the House of Morgan. His emotional plea in that year's presidential election to rescue farmers, new immigrants, and industrial workers from being crucified on "the cross of gold" failed to defeat William McKinley because, until 1901, America was firmly in the hands of the powerful bold entrepreneurs. It would take an assassination to terminate their clout.

Document 1.1. Constitution of the Knights of Labor

As America directed its attention to economic development and urbanization, many people found themselves working in dangerous situations and living in squalid conditions. Accidents on the job, low pay, and 12 hours in the steel mills of Pittsburgh and the oil fields created sharp divisions between the social and economic classes in this nation. Beginning as a secret organization, the Knights of Labor's membership rolls had swelled to 800,000 people by 1886, drawing support from many trades. As mentioned in this chapter, strikers clashed with police in the streets of Chicago that year at Haymarket Square. A bomb was thrown, police died, workers were blamed and killed. The Knights were held responsible for the incident, which had unclear origins, and membership plummeted. But the bleak conditions that had been the focus of the Knights' protests continued during the Gilded Age, and they were replaced by a new labor organization: the American Federation of Labor. The following is an excerpt from the 1878 Preamble of the Constitution of the Knights of Labor.

> The recent alarming development and aggression of aggregated wealth, which, unless checked, will invariably lead to the pauperization and hopeless degradation of the toiling masses, render it imperative, if we desire to enjoy the blessings of life, that a check should be placed upon its power and upon unjust accumulation, and a system adopted which will secure to the laborer the fruits of his toil; and as this much-desired object can only be accomplished by the thorough unification of labor, and the unified efforts of those who obey the divine injunction that "In the sweat of thy brow shalt thou eat bread," we have formed the (Knights of Labor).

Thinking Historically

1. Why did the Captains of Industry consider the Knights of Labor "radical"?
2. How did the organization's acceptance of members from all trades give it strength?
3. Why did its demand for an eight-hour workday (versus the 12-hour workday) worry the Gilded Age's industrialists?
4. What domestic problems were created by long workdays, low wages, and crowded cities?
5. How did the 1886 Haymarket Square Riot destroy the Knights of Labor?

Document 1.2. *Triumphant Democracy*

As this chapter makes clear, Scottish immigrant Andrew Carnegie was one of the most prosperous of the Gilded Age's captains of industry. His steel empire and his alliance with the House of Morgan built our great cities. Carnegie saw conditions differently than the Knights of Labor. He stressed self-help in the accumulation of wealth and the need for all citizens to work zealously to create a great industrialized nation. He almost seemed to be saying to the masses, "be happy with what you have." He wrote of "the Gospel of Wealth," a nation where power and progress took on an almost religious mission. Next, we see his basic philosophy in his 1886 book *Triumphant Democracy*.

> The American citizen has no further need to struggle, being in possession of equality under the laws in every particular. He has not travelled far in the path of genuine Democracy who would not scorn to enjoy a privilege which was not the common birthright of all his fellows.

Thinking Historically

1. Is Carnegie correct in emphasizing the progress taking place in the Gilded Age?
2. Define "genuine Democracy," as Carnegie saw it and as it really existed during the period.
3. What essential points were being ignored by Carnegie as he amassed his personal fortune?
4. What, exactly, is "the Gospel of Wealth"?
5. Is Carnegie naïve in celebrating the end of the "struggle" by people who might toil and be injured in his steel mills?

Document 1.3. *How the Other Half Lives*

Danish immigrant and police reporter Jacob Riis used his journalistic talents to expose the hard living conditions in New York City during the Gilded Age. That metropolis was the capital of the world to the new immigrants who came ashore in the shadow of the Statue of Liberty (see Document 0.1). They arrived with dreams, hoping that on the other side of "the golden door" there would be economic opportunities. Riis wrote about the reality that awaited them: crime, unhealthy living conditions, and low-paying perilous jobs. Rooms could be rented to a family for one dollar a month. He chronicled the crowded ethnic mix in the largest city in America in this excerpt from his 1890 *How the Other Half Lives*.

> When once I asked the agent of a notorious Fourth Ward alley how many people might be living in it I was told: One hundred and forty families, one hundred Irish, thirty-eight Italian, and two that spoke the German tongue. Barring the agent herself there was not a native born-born individual in the court. The answer was characteristic of the cosmopolitan character of lower New York, very nearly so of the whole of it, wherever it runs to alleys and courts. One may find for the asking an Italian, a German, a French, African, Spanish, Bohemian, Russian, Scandinavian, Jewish, and Chinese colony. Even the Arab, who peddles "holy earth" from the Battery as a direct importation from Jerusalem, has his exclusive preserves at the lower end of Washington Street.

Thinking Historically

1. Why did the bold entrepreneurs of the Gilded Age see these "huddled masses" as a means to increase their fortunes?
2. Were there advantages to the ethnic enclaves that arose in New York City?
3. Why did these crowded living conditions serve as sources of crime for Riis to report?
4. What actions should the municipal government have taken to alleviate the city's poverty?
5. Explain how Riis used what he witnessed to become a social reformer?

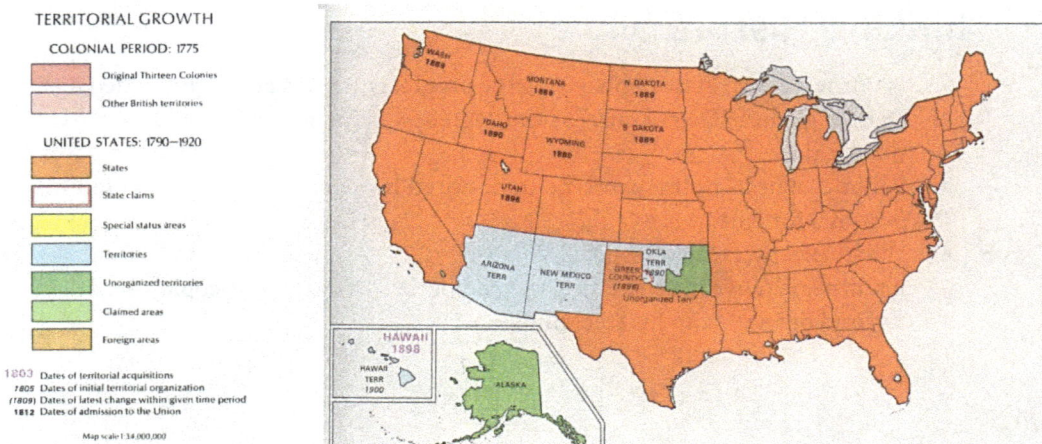

IMG 1.1: Source: http://legacy.lib.utexas.edu/maps/united_states/us_terr_1900.jpg.

Document 1.4. Map of the United States, 1900

As we will see in Chapter 2, the United States by the dawn of the twentieth century had established itself as a world power. Indigenous people surrendered after the 1893 Battle of Wounded Knee, accepting the harsh reality that they had become tenants in what had once been their land. By 1900, there were 193,000 miles of railroad track spanning the continent and transporting goods that made profits for the captains of industry. The United States became the world's largest steel producer, turning out 10,000 tons per year. John D. Rockefeller controlled 90 percent of the nation's refining capacity. America's population in 1900 was 76,000,168, which was a 21 percent increase since 1890, and there were 45 states, excluding the not yet admitted Oklahoma, New Mexico, Arizona, Alaska, and Hawaii. The following map demonstrates the immense country we had become by 1900.

Thinking Historically

1. After reviewing Chapter 1, explain why cities in the eastern United States influenced our economic development during the Gilded Age?
2. Why was New York City so attractive to new immigrants?
3. Why were California and the southwest slower than New York to develop?
4. What lessons should we learn from the story of the decline of Native Americans in the west?
5. Why would our country's future be guided by California and Florida?

THE ARENA

With America industrializing through the wealth of the bold entrepreneurs and the sweat of the huddled masses, we began contemplating an empire that stretched beyond our shores. In 1890, Admiral Alfred Mahan, president of the Naval War College in Rhode Island, published his study titled *The Influence of Sea Power on History*. To him, great nations must construct great navies, which would dominate the oceans. The captains of industry applauded because they and their workers would build a modern navy that would impress the world. Three years later, Professor Frederick Jackson Turner lectured fellow historians about "The frontier in American history." His 1893 address reminded us that one of the themes in our history was constant movement, a restlessness that had swept us across North America, warring with indigenous people, the mother country, and Mexico. Now, in the last decade of the Gilded Age, the continental frontier had been conquered. It was, to the leaders of the time, our destiny to venture into the seas.

The natural richness of Hawaii with its pineapples and strategic harbors became our focus in 1893. With the help of US Marines, we toppled Hawaii's Queen Liliuokalani, creating a protectorate that we could use to reach Asian markets, an attractive goal for American entrepreneurs. Three years later, we focused our attention on the Caribbean, where Spain was trying to cling to the remnants of its decaying empire.

Cuba, 90 miles from Florida, was seeking its independence from Spain. American newspapers, William Randolph Hearst's *New York World* and Joseph Pulitzer's *New York Journal*, focused their attention on Spain's military commander Valeriano Weyler and his detention camps where he incarcerated Cuban rebels. Both papers, typical of Gilded Age publications, vividly reported on the struggle in Cuba, sensationalizing it in what has been called "yellow journalism." Throughout our nation's history, independence has been a powerful theme. Now, in the mid-1890s, newspapers intensified their coverage and shaped the Cuban revolt. Weyler became "Butcher" Weyler, accused of atrocities in the camps. Sometimes, the facts of the revolt got in the way, angering Spain, which considered us meddlesome.

The last of the Gilded Age presidents, William McKinley, was elected in 1896. He was allied with the captains of industry and became immersed in what was occurring in Cuba. In 1897, the Spanish ambassador to Washington, Enrique Marquis de Lome, wrote his superiors a secret note that was highly critical of the president, who de Lome labeled "a would be politician" with "feet of clay." The diplomatic correspondence came into the possession of American newspapers, which published it, enflaming the Cuban situation. McKinley, seeking to display strength, sent one of our new cruisers, *U.S.S. Maine*, to Cuba against Spanish wishes. In Havana Harbor in early 1898, the vessel exploded, killing 262 American sailors and propelling us toward war with Spain, which professed its noninvolvement in the sinking of the *Maine*.

By April 1898, McKinley was granted a congressional declaration of war. The nation shouted, "Remember the Maine" while the newspapers called for revenge. Interestingly, recent research has proven the sinking to be an accident caused by a coal fire. Assistant Secretary of the Navy Theodore Roosevelt ordered the American fleet toward the Philippines, another part of Spain's empire. Moving quickly, Roosevelt resigned his position in the administration and helped organize a group known as "the Rough Riders," who after brief training would head to Cuba to liberate it. Roosevelt became a hero by courageously attacking Kettle and San Juan hills in what he would herald as "one crowded hour." The war with Spain would be what Secretary of State John Hay called "a splendid little war." It turned Roosevelt into a legend and resulted in the creation, by the 1899 Treaty of Paris, of an empire: the Philippines, Guam, Puerto Rico, and congressional oversight of newly independent Cuba.

During the presidential election year of 1900, McKinley added Roosevelt to the ticket as vice president. Roosevelt had returned from the war to serve briefly as New York's governor, fearlessly challenging the captains of industry. Now, as vice president, he became what one critic reminded the entrepreneurs "only one heartbeat away from the presidency." That "heartbeat" was stilled within months when McKinley, visiting the World's Fair in Buffalo, New York, was mortally wounded by Leon Czogosy, an anarchist. As the new century began, it would be 42-year-old Theodore Roosevelt, reformer, who began the Progressive Era.

Roosevelt declared war on what he called "bigness." He called for a Square Deal for all Americans, and invited Booker T. Washington to dine with him at the White House; he began trying to break up the monopolies (the trusts). The Gilded Age had been replaced by an assertive president who inserted himself into domestic and foreign affairs. By 1904, he had supported a revolution in the South American nation of Colombia, slicing off the northern part of the country, Panama, and began the decade-long construction of the Panama Canal. As the president explained, "I let Congress talk while I took the canal."

In 1904, as he sought election in his own name, Roosevelt announced the Roosevelt Corollary to the Monroe Doctrine, a bold diplomatic statement that the Western Hemisphere was the responsibility of the United States, and we would patrol it and collect any debts. European nations should forget about our part of the world. He won the election and followed it with regulation measures, such as the 1906 Food and Drug Act. The government now was battling the trusts and seeking to provide safer food and drugs. That year, he hosted Russian and Japanese diplomats and hammered out a peace that ended the Russo-Japanese War, earning for himself the Nobel Peace Prize.

Roosevelt, who had spent time in the Dakotas after the death of his first wife while he was in his early 20s, focused his energies on preserving much of the west for future generations. He considered the establishment of the National Park Service as his greatest achievement, but he had many. In 1907, he sent the Great White Fleet, a score of new American vessels, on a world tour, trying to symbolize his peaceful intentions. He reminded the world, however, that he followed the African adage, "Speak softly and carry a big stick." While Americans loved his progressivism and his assertiveness, he honored a pledge he had made in 1904: he would not seek another term in the White House. Nonetheless, he handpicked his successor, William Howard Taft, who had served as our governor of the Philippines, subduing people who mistakenly thought the war with Spain would result in their own independence.

While Roosevelt went off to hunt wild game in Africa, Taft, an attorney, kept "trust-busting" the economic monopolies. But in 1910, Taft fired the director of the National Park Service, Gifford Pinchot, who had been selected by Roosevelt to manage the thousands of acres that had been set aside for public parks. This action created a huge rift between Roosevelt and Taft. The two old allies challenged each other for the presidency for the Republican Party nomination in 1912, wrecking party unity with Roosevelt forming "the Bull Moose" or Progressive Party. This situation enabled the governor of New Jersey, Democrat Woodrow Wilson, to triumph.

Wilson, a former university professor, issued his progressive program: the New Freedom. Unfortunately, the native-born southerner also racially segregated the government and prevented giving women the vote. Compounding his challenges were war clouds that were forming in Europe. He professed "neutrality" when the Great War commenced in 1914 between the Allies and the Central Powers. He pledged in 1916 as he ran for reelection that he would not send America's sons to foreign wars. By then, however, the Germans, members of the Central Powers, were unleashing their submarines on allied ships, resulting in the deaths of many American passengers.

Despite his earlier promises of "neutrality," Wilson was outraged in early 1917 to learn of the Zimmerman Telegram, a questionable document in which Germany supposedly offered Mexico the return of the southwestern United States (land that it had lost in the Mexican War) if it would distract Americans from aiding the Allies. Wilson, talking about freedom of the seas and safety for Americans on the oceans from submarine attacks, received a declaration of war in the spring of that year. America, significantly, would enter the Great War as an Associated Power of the Allies. The infusion of fresh troops, nonetheless, tilted the balance on the battlefields in favor of the Allies.

With the war still raging, Wilson issued in January 1918 his Fourteen Points, an idealistic plan for eventual world peace with no secret treaties, self-determination of people, and a League of Nations to prevent future wars. By November, the Allies and the sole Associated Power had exhausted the enemy, and an armistice occurred. At the 1919 Paris Peace Conference, Wilson lobbied his fellow victors to adopt the Fourteen Points, but they were in no mood to treat the Central Powers fairly, stripping them of territory; forcing them to pay the winners reparations, which we refused; and demanding that they accept total guilt for the war. Wilson did get approval for his League of Nations.

While the peace conference was taking place, a global pandemic, the Spanish flu, was killing 50,000,000 people worldwide (650,000 in America), more than the Great War itself. This pandemic killed young people in their prime, an age group that had already been decimated by the war. Wilson returned from the conference and encountered stiff Senate opposition to ratification of the treaty. An exhausted president crisscrossed the nation urging support for his vision of making this war the war to end all wars, as he explained. In 1919, while on this tour, he suffered a debilitating stroke and mental fatigue. Rushing the ill president back to the White House, First Lady Edith Wilson and the president's physician shielded the public from the truth about his dire condition. He had become, in a sense, a casualty of the Great War.

The Progressive Era ended with a nation weary of war, influenza, and a disabled president. The Nineteenth Amendment to the Constitution was ratified in 1920, giving the ballot to women. The previous amendment put in place Prohibition, which prevented manufacturing, transportation, and sale of alcoholic beverages. Many in this exhausted nation, nevertheless, were searching for what would be called "normalcy" and some looseness. They would get plenty of both in the Roaring 20s.

Document 2.1. Beveridge's Address to Congress

Thirty-seven-year-old Senator Albert J. Beveridge of Ohio was an enthusiastic supporter of America assuming a major role on the world stage. It was a new century, and the United States had a new mission: proudly marching across the globe spreading our influence on every nation that stood in our way. The senator saw this zeal as our destiny, and in 1900, he spoke to his congressional colleagues about his dream that democracy, American-style, was just what the twentieth century needed. Our flag was moving eastward. This excerpt makes clear that Beveridge was not going to be deterred in his quest.

> Mr. President, the times call for candor. The Philippines are ours forever, "territory belonging to the United States," as the Constitution calls them. And just beyond the Philippines are China's illimitable markets. We will not retreat from either. We will not repudiate our duty in the archipelago. We will not abandon our opportunity in the Orient. We will not renounce

our part in the mission of our race, trustee, under God, of the civilization of the world.

Thinking Historically

1. Explain Beveridge's belief that civilization would be enhanced if we led the way.
2. How was the march of our flag a positive thing to Asians, who by 1920, were becoming subject to immigration quotas in America?
3. What might occur if Asian nations resisted America's destiny?
4. What opportunities were we seeking in the Orient?
5. Comment on the racist tone of Beveridge as the twentieth century started.

Document 2.2. "The Man in the Arena"

As this chapter makes clear, Theodore Roosevelt was a bundle of energy, a war hero who rose by accident to the presidency. The 1901 assassination of William McKinley helped end the reign of the captains of industry and begin the Progressive Era, a time of reform with America active on the world stage, with Theodore Roosevelt at the helm. After he left the White House in 1909, he headed to Africa on a safari which brought back to America's museums hundreds of mounted wild game. In 1910, he paused in Europe to visit various countries. The following is part of his "The Man in the Arena" speech that year at Paris' Sorbonne.

> It is not the critic who counts; not the man who points out how strong man stumbles, or where the door of deeds could have done them better. The credit belongs to the man who is actually in the arena, whose face is marred by dust and sweat and blood; who strives valiantly; who errs, who comes short again and again, because there is no effort without error and shortcoming; but who does actually strive to do the deeds; who knows great enthusiasms, the great devotions; who spends himself in a worthy cause.

Thinking Historically

1. Is Theodore Roosevelt speaking of individual human beings or our nation?
2. How do his 1910 remarks explain the American global mission of the twentieth century?
3. Did Roosevelt's aggressive tone help or harm America's image among the nations of the world?
4. Do you see irony in the fact that during his presidency, Roosevelt kept us out of foreign wars, winning the Nobel Peace Prize in 1906?
5. Do you think Roosevelt during his European tour detected the world's slide toward war?

Document 2.3. Woodrow Wilson's Declaration of War

By 1914, much of the world had ensnared itself in entangling treaties of alliance, almost eager to go to war with each other. Territorial ambitions and ancient ethnic hatreds were ignited in 1914 when the crown prince of Austria-Hungary was assassinated by a Serb nationalist. Woodrow Wilson professed our neutrality as the Great War began, trying to walk a thin line between the Allies and Central Powers as this chapter describes, selling weapons to both combatants. Unrestricted submarine warfare by Germany resulted in American deaths on targeted British vessels. In 1917, despite his promise in the previous year's election, President Wilson requested a congressional declaration of war to ensure "freedom of the seas." The following is an excerpt from his war request.

> On the third of February last I officially laid before you the extraordinary announcement of the Imperial German Government that on and after the first of February it was its purpose to put aside all restraints of law or of humanity and use its submarines to sink every vessel that sought to approach either the ports of Great Britain and Ireland or the western coasts of Europe or any of the ports controlled by the enemies of Germany within the Mediterranean.

Thinking Historically

1. Was the United States favoring the Allies before Wilson requested this declaration of war?
2. How did Germany and the other Central Powers view Wilson's professed "neutrality"?
3. Voting against war, Representative Jeanette Rankin of Montana said, "In times of war it is the women who pay the supreme price." What did she mean?
4. Why would the United States be an Associated Power in the war?
5. Did Wilson clearly understand Germany's decision to use unrestricted submarine warfare?

Document 2.4. Paris Peace Conference Map, 1919

The Great War, which began in the Balkans with hatred between Austria and Serbian nationalists, quickly escalated into a major conflict, engulfing the world. While Americans did not officially enter the war until 1917 (see Document 2.3), Woodrow Wilson hoped to make it "the war to end all wars." The conflict redrew the map and set the

Chapter 2 THE ARENA   13

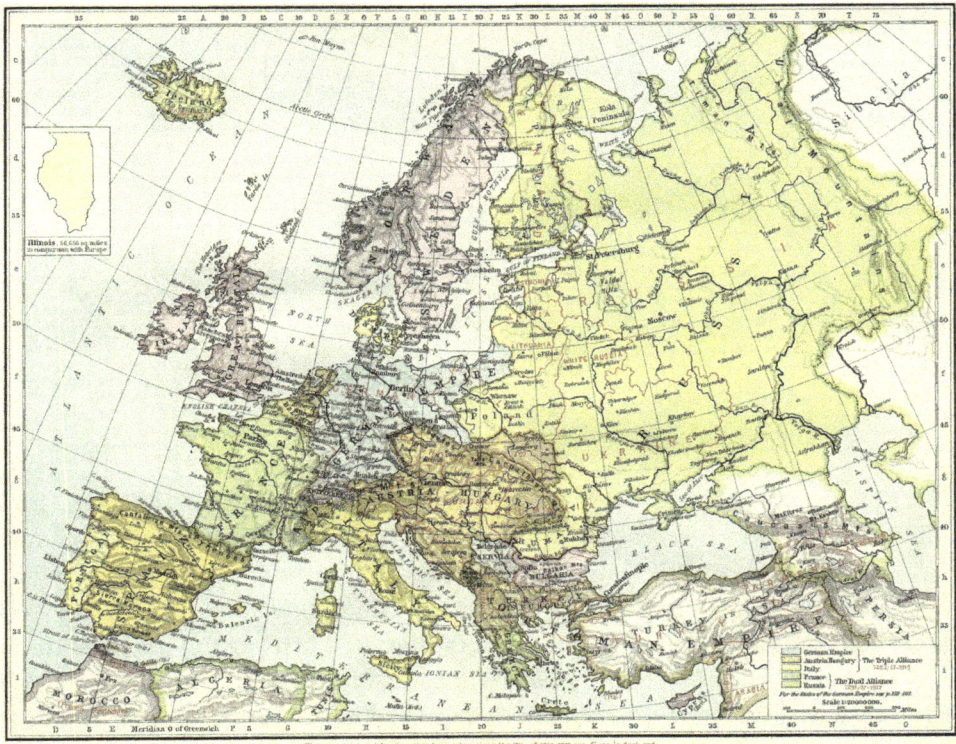

IMG 2.1: Source: https://commons.wikimedia.org/wiki/File:Europe_1918.jpg.

stage for World War II, a much larger conflagration. Study the map that follows and ponder the tensions that the Great War and the 1919 Paris Peace Conference discussed in this chapter created.

Thinking Historically

1. Was Wilson naïve about the ethnic forces at play in the Great War?
2. Did the breaking up of Austria's empire create acrimony that burst forth a generation later?
3. Why did our president fail to establish lasting peace in 1919?
4. Did the harsh treatment of the war's losers at the Paris Peace Conference create the later rise of dictators?
5. Why does this chapter observe that Wilson, himself, became a casualty of the Great War?

3

LOOSENESS

The horrors of the Great War redrew the world's map, demolishing the empires of the losers: Austria-Hungary, Germany, and the Ottoman Empire. Colonies controlled by these nations were redistributed to the victorious Allies. The seeds of World War II were sown at the 1919 Paris Peace Conference as Germany was forced to demilitarize, to accept total guilt for the Great War, and to pay reparations to the winners. As we saw in the previous chapter, President Woodrow Wilson tried earnestly to create a world of peace, but the ethnic hatred and anger at Germany made his dream impossible. France, Great Britain, and Italy outflanked the idealistic American president as they tried to neuter Germany as a world power.

Our country's involvement in the Great War came late. Wilson did not request a declaration of war until the spring of 1917 (see Document 2.3). Our troops did, nonetheless, pay a significant human cost in the conflict, losing 130,000 men in combat with an additional 203,460 wounded. A new word entered the vocabulary, "shell shock," the psychological damage done to men in combat. Erich Maria Remarque in his novel *All Quiet on The Western Front* wrote of life in the trenches, the squalor, and death. It was, indeed, history's first modern war: airplanes, submarines, poison gas, men struggling to cross a no-man's-land between combatants dazed by the death all around them.

Compounding the bleakness of the Great War was the Spanish flu epidemic, an avian-caused pandemic, which ironically did not originate in Spain. This illness cost 650,000 American lives from 1918 through 1919, targeting the young, a generation already decimated by the war. Worldwide 50,000,000 lives were lost to this pandemic, coming on the heels of the Great War, which had cost more than 41,000,000 lives. The world, by 1920, was exhausted, and in this nation, a decade-long period of escapism, of looseness began.

The presidential election of 1920 was largely managed by the victor's campaign aid, Mark Hanna, who boasted that he would market Ohio's Warren G. Harding, a US senator, "like a bar of soap." Harding was handsome, tanned, cheerful, and said little about the challenges facing the world. He liked to "bloviate," speaking of insignificant matters but promising to focus America's attention inward (see Document 3.1). Harding called for "normalcy," a return to America first, and a rejection of Wilson's interest in international affairs. He would bring with him to the White House "the Ohio Gang," cronies who would carouse with him in violation of Prohibition and take advantage of their friendship with the new president, looting the government in a series of scandals (the most significant was Teapot Dome, a federal reserve where the Harding friends drilled for oil) but which would not be revealed until after Harding's death in 1923. The good times were rolling, and they started with the excesses of Harding (who fathered an illegitimate daughter) and the Ohio Gang.

Throughout the Roaring 20s, as they are sometimes called, there was a burst of artistic creativity and cultural awareness coming out of New York: the Harlem Renaissance. Poets like Langston Hughes and Countee Cullen, folklorist Zora Neale Hurston, and writers like James Weldon Johnson (who wrote the African American National Anthem "Lift Every Voice and Sing") left their mark on the era, as did musicians like Duke Ellington and Louis Armstrong and the voice of Josephine Baker. Dancers filled the floors of the Savoy Club and the Cotton Club, forgetting the terrors of the war years and immersing themselves in jazz.

The National Association for the Advancement of Colored People (NAACP), a civil rights organization, had been founded in 1909 by W.E.B. Du Bois and others to address lynching and other injustices, and the Universal Negro Improvement Association began in 1916 under Marcus Garvey, advocating a return to African pride and Black entrepreneurship. But racism was tenacious in the 1920s, and censorship of acting by Paul Robeson, a talented singer, and the light-skinned actress Fredi Washington illustrates that prejudice was powerful even in the movies because the Ku Klux Klan disapproved of anything that seemed permissive (see Document 3.2).

The decade's literature was shaped by F. Scott Fitzgerald, who was accompanied by his wife, Zelda. Fitzgerald set the tone with his 1920 novel *This Side of Paradise* and the 1925 *The Great Gatsby*. Both works were full of carefree young characters, dancing and drinking gin. College students in the books participated in "petting parties," where a new type of woman, "the flapper," made her appearance. With bobbed hair, loose beaded dresses, and red lipstick, the flappers held their own with their male counterparts, enjoying parties held at the mysterious Jay Gatsby's lavish estate (Document 3.3).

While Henry Ford's Model T was unveiled a decade earlier, this automobile roared across America in the 1920s. Ford priced the vehicle in the reach of the masses ($550 for a 1914 Touring Car and $295 for a sedan) and pledged, "The customer can have it any color he wants as long as he wants it black." By 1925, Ford's plants turned out 16 cars a minute and paid assembly-line workers $5.00 per day as Ford preached his philosophy (Document 3.4). Young people climbed into the vehicles and headed for evenings dancing the Charleston at clubs and sampling gin at "speakeasies," establishments where alcohol was sold in violation of Prohibition. One critical judge called automobiles, "Houses of prostitution on wheels."

Hostility toward new immigrants manifested in legislation limiting Chinese immigration in 1924. The Statue of Liberty's golden door had been slammed shut. Earlier in the decade, a paymaster was murdered in South Braintree, Massachusetts. The Italian immigrants, Sacco and Vanzetti, were blamed for the death, even though there was flimsy evidence about the role played by Vanzetti. The judge, Webster Thayer, spewed hate and prejudice toward both men, and both were executed in 1927. The nativism of the era, as mentioned earlier, had broadened its reach beyond African Americans to ensnare anyone different from the White Anglo-Saxon Protestant population. Even John T. Scopes, a Tennessee substitute teacher, met with resistance for teaching evolution in 1925, a challenge to those who favored only the teaching of Biblical creationism.

In 1927, Charles Lindbergh, a Minnesota airmail pilot, flew his plane, the *Spirit of St. Louis*, solo nonstop from New York to Paris. This spectacular feat became international front-page news, earning hero status for "Lucky Lindy," and demonstrated America's quest for new frontiers, this time in the skies over the Atlantic Ocean.

Throughout the 1920s, there had been a looseness to politics. The corrupt Harding administration was followed upon his death in 1923 with the casual, *laissez-faire* approach of Calvin Coolidge. "Keep cool with Coolidge," Americans said. He said, "the business of America is business." And the economy, largely unregulated, reached the boiling point by 1929. The stock market collapsed that October, easy credit knocked the solvency from beneath capitalism, 5,000 banks found their vaults empty, and depositors were ruined; durable goods like refrigerators had been overproduced, farmers battled droughts and insects, Germany defaulted on its war reparations, our new president Herbert Hoover (see Chapter 4) was unable to respond to the severe economic situation, and the looseness of the decade was replaced by the hangover of the Great Depression.

Document 3.1. Warren G. Harding's Inaugural Address

Ohio senator Warren G. Harding, his able campaign manager Mark Hanna, and watchful wife Florence Harding marketed the Republican presidential nominee in 1920 as the perfect antidote to the Great War and the Spanish flu epidemic. Harding, with his salt-and-pepper hair and perpetual tan, looked presidential, pleasantly smiling and heading to the golf courses and speakeasies with the Ohio Gang, who, as noted in this chapter, looted America during the Harding administration. His 1921 inaugural address, excerpted next, gives us a glimpse of his plans for noninvolvement in world affairs.

> The recorded progress of our Republic, materially and spiritually, in itself proves the wisdom of the inherited policy of noninvolvement in Old World affairs. Confident of our ability to work out our own destiny, and jealously guarding our right to do so, we seek no part in directing the destinies of the Old World. We do not mean to be entangled. We will accept no responsibility except as our own conscience and judgment, in each instance, may determine.

Thinking Historically

1. Contrast the approach to foreign affairs of Woodrow Wilson and Warren G. Harding.

2. Why was Harding's return to "normalcy" so popular among the electorate?
3. Why does Harding seem perfect for the mood of the Roaring 1920s?
4. Comment on how America's failure to join the League of Nations contributed to later international crises.
5. What fundamental point does Harding not comprehend about the world after the Great War?

Document 3.2. The Klan's Fight for Americanism

The Ku Klux Klan of the 1920s reached beyond the South and aimed at "aliens" "infesting" America after the Great War. While Woodrow Wilson had criticized the communists who had created the Soviet Union during the Revolution of 1917, the Klan took this hatred much further. It boasted 3,000,000 members by 1926 and grew across the nation. The enemies that the "new" Ku Klux Klan identified were Jews, Catholics, new immigrants, communists, and Blacks. Its robed members marched in the capital and claimed political power in states from Indiana to Georgia. In the following excerpt, Klan leader Hiram W. Evans, a Texas dentist, explains his view that the Klan was a reaction to modern America's excesses.

> The Klan, therefore, has now come to speak for the great mass of Americans of the old pioneer stock. We believe that it does fairly and faithfully represent them, and that our proof lies in their support. To understand the Klan, then, it is necessary to understand the character and present mind of the old-stock Americans. The mass, it must be remembered, as distinguished from the intellectually mongrelized "Liberals."

Thinking Historically

1. Explain the support that the "new" Klan of the 1920s had beyond the South.
2. What was it about the new immigrants that angered Evans?
3. Why did "old-stock" Americans join the Klan?
4. What differentiates this resurrected Ku Klux Klan from the earlier organization of the Reconstruction Era?
5. Even though the "new" Klan went dormant after a sex scandal involving its Indiana leader, why is it still a presence in modern America?

Document 3.3. *The Great Gatsby*

As this chapter notes, F. Scott Fitzgerald's novels captured the looseness of the 1920s as young Americans searched for a form of relief. His 1920 *This Side of Paradise* and *The Great Gatsby* of 1925 created a carefree mood with flappers and partiers dancing to jazz and drinking as readers escaped, for a while, from the serious problems facing the country and the world in the decade. The following is an excerpt from *The Great Gatsby* describing the beautiful character Daisy Buchanan's encounter with the smitten narrator, Nick Carraway.

> Under the dripping bare lilac-trees a large open car was coming up the drive. It stopped. Daisy's face, tipped sideways, beneath a three-cornered lavender hat looked at me with a bright ecstatic smile.
> "Is this absolutely where you live, my dearest one?"
> The exhilarating ripple of her voice was a wild tonic in the rain. I had to follow the sound of it for a moment, up and down, with my ear alone, before any words came through. A damp streak of hair lay like a dash of blue paint across her cheek, and her hand was wet with glistening drops as I took it to help her from the car.
> "Are you in love with me," she said low in my ear, "or why did I have to come alone?"

Thinking Historically

1. How did Fitzgerald's characters represent the seductive looseness of the 1920s?
2. Compare the literature of the decade with modern standards. Has it remained timeless?
3. Does Daisy Buchanan come across in this excerpt as vacuous or calculating?
4. Why did the never-ending parties at Jay Gatsby's estate appeal to a generation escaping the horrors of the Great War?
5. Explain the popularity of Fitzgerald's novels.

Document 3.4. Henry Ford's Philosophy

As Chapter 3 explains, Henry Ford's assembly-line-produced automobiles are representative of the theme of America on the move. His business model was mass-produced affordable vehicles priced within reach of many Americans. His philosophy, excerpted next from a 1928 article, was based on his belief that his creation would propel our nation into the future and strengthen capitalism.

> People who try to understand only the immediate times are somewhat behind the times. Signs of the times, then, are the signs of things to come. The signs of the times that now are were given long ago. By the time they emerge into actuality they are no longer signs, they are the times themselves. It is one thing to see a thing, another thing to see through a thing. There is very little of life on the surface. We see today as the product of distant yesterdays; yet hidden in today is a root of distant tomorrows, and it is the man who knows the coming tomorrows who really sees most of life.

Thinking Historically

1. Was Henry Ford a visionary or just lucky to be at the helm of his car company?
2. How did his affordable automobiles propel America into the future?
3. Why were other more expensive vehicles unable to compete with Ford's models?
4. What, exactly, did Ford mean by his comment, "There is very little of life on the surface"?
5. Describe the "distant tomorrows" that Ford's brand of capitalism mentions.

4

THE GREATEST GENERATION

A self-made millionaire who had traveled the globe as a mining engineer, Iowa's Herbert Hoover had witnessed unrest in 1899 in China during the Boxer Rebellion. In the aftermath of the Great War, he developed a plan for feeding the hungry of Europe. During the Harding administration, Hoover served as secretary of commerce, avoiding the taint of that presidency's corruption. His triumph in 1928 over New York governor Al Smith, a Roman Catholic and a "wet" on the issue of Prohibition, seemed to be a fitting continuation to the decade's "normalcy." The previous year, Congress had ratified the Kellogg-Briand Pact, which forbade future wars, and there was great anticipation that the "Great Engineer" would preside over further peace and economic prosperity.

But by 1929, the excesses and the looseness of the Roaring 1920s undermined the vitality of the nation's economy: weak oversight of the banks and the stock market, combined with easy consumer credit, problems in agriculture, overproduction of durable goods that lacked markets, and Germany's inability to pay its reparations to the victors in the Great War. Thus, the world plunged into an economic morass just as Hoover took office.

Human suffering, lost jobs and homes, uninsured bank accounts, evaporated stock market profits, foreclosed upon farms, hunger, and hopelessness paralyzed America, and the president seemed unable to exercise leadership in a time of immense crisis.

Hoover believed that the economy, given time, would correct itself, but time had run out for many citizens.

As the 1930s began, things only got worse. In Alabama, a group of nine African American youths, hoping to find employment, stowed away on a train heading out of Scottsboro. Two white women were hiding in the same railroad car. When train detectives discovered the freeloaders, the females accused the Scottsboro Boys, aged 13 to 19, of rape. The 1931 trial, broadcast nationally on the new device of radio combined race and sex and produced guilty verdicts for the youths, even though years later the females divulged that no crime had occurred.

As the Great Depression deepened, the Great Engineer supported making federal assistance available to America's top firms, but the people suffering were not in board rooms. They were hiding in railroad cars, or riding in caravans heading west to California in search of opportunities as John Steinbeck's novel *The Grapes of Wrath* chronicled, or marching on Washington seeking payment of a bonus that had been pledged by Congress to veterans of the Great War. These Bonus Marchers, 17,000 strong, were desperate men who had families to feed. The "bonus" had been promised in 1945, but in the summer of 1932, these veterans urgently needed the $1,000 payments immediately.

Again, Hoover seemed unable to abandon his fundamental belief that the economy would right itself and suffering would be alleviated without bold government intervention. The "private sector" was sufficient, Hoover maintained. The "bonus" would be paid in 1945 as the initial legislation mandated, the president explained. The Bonus Marchers built camps in Washington, visited the capitol itself, and begged for accelerated payment. Hoover ordered army chief of staff General Douglas MacArthur to remove the veterans from federal property. The general, saying he "smelled revolution in the air," charged the marchers, throwing them into disarray, killing two, burning their shacks, and dooming any hope the Great Engineer had to win reelection in 1932.

New York State had been creatively addressing the Great Depression at the state level under the leadership of Governor Franklin D. Roosevelt. As Document 4.1 shows us, there was desperation flowing across the land. Charities and churches were unable to meet the human need. Roosevelt promised a New Deal, a fresh approach by the government to the misery. Activism, reform, regulation were needed, and after the debacle of the Bonus March, it was accepted by many, except the incumbent president, who clung to his belief that only the large companies still operating deserved government assistance, that Franklin D. Roosevelt (FDR), the charismatic and optimistic Democratic Party nominee, could deliver on a fundamental restructuring of the federal government.

The November 1932 election was a landslide for Roosevelt and his team of advisers, the Brain Trust, who would deliver something very different to the American people. The results were 42 states for FDR and 6 for Hoover. The Democrat received 472 electoral votes, while the Republicans earned only 59. The United States impatiently awaited the New Deal during the interregnum, the time from November's election to the inauguration in March 1933. Even an attempted assassination of Roosevelt during a Miami visit in February failed to dampen the sea of anticipation that awaited America.

Roosevelt's Brain Trust, talented professors, social workers, and experts on labor, agriculture, and banking commenced the Hundred Days, a whirlwind of legislation that Congress overwhelmingly endorsed. Banks, those still open, were examined and reopened with insurance of deposits guaranteed. The stock market would be closely monitored. Farmers would be paid not to produce crops, driving payments upward. Codes for industries would be offered to regulate work hours and increase pay. Members of Congress took pay cuts. The government economized, tightening its own belt. Alphabet agencies were born: the Civilian Conservation Corps (CCC) and the Tennessee Valley Authority (TVA). The former paid unemployed young males to fight forest fires, plant trees, and build parks for one dollar per day. The latter initiative dammed the Tennessee River, producing electricity and jobs.

The Hundred Days did not solve the Great Depression, but it gave evidence that a New Deal had arrived. Roosevelt added to his congressional support in the 1934 midterm elections. Some critics said he did not go far enough. Louisiana Senator Huey Long advocated for a redistribution of wealth where "every man was a king." California physician Francis Townshend lobbied for assistance for the elderly. Roosevelt responded in 1935 with the massive Works Progress Administration, which employed people in public works projects, such as building courthouses and city halls. Artists painted murals; historians interviewed aged former slaves and compiled cemetery records. Social Security was enacted to create a modest safety net for older Americans. The National Labor Relations Board gave labor increased power in the workplace.

Roosevelt won a second term in 1936, continuing to recharge the depleted battery of America. He and First Lady Eleanor Roosevelt traveled the land, urging public support for the New Deal. But war clouds began to appear on the horizon. Benito Mussolini and his Italian fascists had come to power in 1922, attempting to produce a new Roman Empire. In 1935, Mussolini had attacked Ethiopia, and the League of Nations, which the United States had never joined, stood idly by. In Germany, Adolph Hitler had come to power in 1933, the same year as FDR. He and his Nazis rearmed in violation of the agreement at the 1919 Paris Peace Conference. The Soviet Union's Joseph Stalin consolidated communist authority in Russia.

In the east, the Japanese military, with the acquiescence of Emperor Hirohito, marauded into Asia, brutalizing the Chinese. The 1937 Rape of Nanking is one example of the horrors the Japanese inflicted on the mainland. Here, Congress passed a series of Neutrality Acts, restricting the president. FDR objected, but the scars of the Great War were still fresh. By 1938, Hitler had annexed Austria and gobbled up Czechoslovakia as the United Kingdom and France weakly appeased him. Mussolini annexed Albania the following year. And Hitler and Stalin signed a nonaggression pact that divided Poland and gave Stalin the Baltic nations. The ravages of the Great Depression occupied us as the world tumbled toward another war. Roosevelt spoke about the importance of liberty and human rights, but most Americans were more concerned with their own anemic domestic situations.

When Hitler invaded Poland in 1939, the United Kingdom and France responded with war, but it was nearly too late. An alliance between Germany, Italy, and Japan (the Axis Powers) had been established. The Nazis drove eastward into Belgium and the Netherlands. In 1940, Hitler toppled France, and the United Kingdom and its new prime minister, Winston Churchill, sought American aid. Congress continued to be reluctant to abandon neutrality; some Americans, like the aviation hero Charles Lindbergh, urged a policy of America First. Roosevelt did, however, persuade Congress to enact a bases for destroyers deal with Churchill, supplying badly needed vessels to the British as the Nazis launched nightly aerial attacks on Great Britain.

The decade of the 1930s ended with America still mired in the Great Depression. John Steinbeck's 1939 aforementioned novel *The Grapes of Wrath* chronicles the bank-foreclosed

Joad family's odyssey to reach California from Oklahoma where, they believed, jobs awaited them. That journey was played out in real life throughout the decade, frantic and desperate people moving west in search of jobs, food, and hope. With a global war occurring, two world fairs were held in 1939: one in San Francisco and one in New York. The former showcased the newly completed Golden Gate Bridge and a man-made island called "The World of Tomorrow." The New York event unveiled the General Electric display of television, new technology that would assist the war effort when we found ourselves in the conflict.

Roosevelt secured an unprecedented third term in 1940, warning the electorate about the demons marching across the globe. Hitler and Mussolini had by that time tried out their new planes and weapons in the Spanish Civil War from 1936 through 1939. Roosevelt used all of his legislative talents to loosen our neutrality, offering Churchill in 1941 a lend-lease program, supplying the beleaguered United Kingdom with badly needed supplies. Conscription was approved narrowly by the United States Congress, and maneuvers took place in the southern states. But we were ill-prepared for a second world war because the Great Depression had sapped our strength.

During the summer of 1941, Hitler turned on his chum Stalin and attacked the Soviet Union, advancing toward Moscow, where the frightened Soviets scrambled to move the embalmed body of their founder, V.I. Lenin, to safety. The Japanese did horrific things to civilians in China, Korea, and Southeast Asia. We refused to sell oil or scrap metal to the Japanese military, an action that Japan considered an act of war. On December 7, the Japanese launched a surprise attack on the American naval base at Pearl Harbor, Hawaii. Nearly 3,000 Americans lost their lives as two waves of Japanese planes sunk our fleet on a Sunday morning. The next day, the president called for a congressional war declaration; he told America it was "a date which will live in infamy."

The Americans now joined the United Kingdom, the Free French, the Chinese, and the Soviet Union, an alliance that shared common enemies. Stalin urged an allied invasion in Nazi-held France, which would distract Hitler, who had advanced to the outskirts of Moscow. This Second Front would not be opened until 1944 as the United States battled tenacious Japan in the Pacific Theater. Every American mobilized for the war that had now come for us. Women enlisted in special units, and the mythical Rosie the Riveter filled in for males who now fought in the Pacific. One of the early measures FDR took in 1942 was rounding up the Nisei, second-generation Japanese Americans who, in the aftermath of Pearl Harbor, were suspected of espionage. Forced to sell their West Coast businesses and homes quickly, the Nisei were incarcerated in detention camps for the remainder of the war. Ironically, some were drafted and served heroically in the American Armed Forces.

The Second Front, an attack on Nazi-held France, occurred in the summer of 1944. An allied invasion force of Americans, British, and Canadians came ashore on D-Day, June 6, meeting the Free French. The allied commander was General Dwight Eisenhower. This bold military effort turned the tide of the war in Europe as Stalin attacked the Nazis from the east, and the other allies pushed inward from Normandy's beaches. In the Pacific, the Americans were making progress on the numerous islands held by Japan. Mussolini was toppled by Italian partisans and allied forces, executed by his fellow Italians. The tide was turning for those who had united against some of history's most brutal forces.

Shortly after Pearl Harbor, Roosevelt assembled scientists and engineers to begin the development of the Manhattan Project, a top-secret effort to build a deadly atomic bomb. Roosevelt kept this project secret as the personnel worked to harness the power of the atom. He secured reelection in 1944, but in April 1945, after a meeting in Yalta two months earlier with Churchill and Stalin, FDR died in Warm Springs, Georgia. His successor, Vice President Harry Truman, was now briefed on the Manhattan Project as Americans fought the Japanese in several bloody battles on their way to the mainland of Japan.

In his Berlin bunker, Hitler committed suicide in May as the American and Soviet military tightened the noose on the Nazi regime. Truman turned his attention on the Pacific Theater, witnessing the fight-to-the-death efforts of the Japanese and suicide aerial attacks by Japanese kamikaze planes loaded with explosives as they sought out American ships. Receiving reports from the successful experiments being conducted by the Manhattan Project team, the president gave instructions "to release when ready." The first atomic bomb fell on Hiroshima on August 6, killing more than 110,000 Japanese. The second bomb was detonated at Nakasaki three days later, killing more than 75,000 Japanese. Harry Truman saw his decision as a way to save American and Japanese lives.

As the Japanese formally surrendered aboard the *USS Missouri* the following month, the Greatest Generation, those Americans who had endured the hard times of the Great Depression and four years of combat on faraway battlefields had been victorious. Hitler and Mussolini were dead; the Japanese emperor had to admit he was not divine, and his military had surrendered. But almost immediately a new conflict, a Cold War between America and the Soviet Union, emerged. The World War II alliance between the two nations had vanished, replaced by conflict in a dangerous world with nuclear weapons.

Document 4.1. *Hard Times*

The abyss of the Great Depression was a deep catastrophe affecting all regions of the United States and workers from most professions. Unemployment reached more than 20% by 1932 with bread lines forming, empty bank vaults, parched fields, and homeless families huddled in makeshift shelters in what were called "Hoovervilles." In his oral history of the era entitled *Hard Times*, Chicago journalist Studs Terkel quotes one African American lamenting, "The Negro was born in depression. It didn't mean too much to him." The population as a whole, however, felt the despair of the collapsed economy, society, and political system. In the following January 1932 excerpt from a female Minnesotan, we sense the toll on human beings as they waited for scarce relief.

> I am sitting in the city free employment bureau. It's the woman's section. We have been sitting here now for four hours. We sit here every day, waiting for a job. There are no jobs. Most of us have had no breakfast. Some have had scant rations for over a year. Hunger makes a human being

lapse into a state of lethargy, especially city hunger. Is there any place else in the world where a human being is supposed to go hungry amidst plenty without an outcry, without protest, where only the boldest steal or kill for bread, and the timid crawl the streets, hunger like the beak of a terrible bird at the vitals?

Thinking Historically

1. Were conditions in America's cities more critical than on the farms?
2. By 1932, the dire situation faced by many citizens had gone on three years. Was America close to a revolution?
3. Was there a growing clash between the people who had the essentials and those sitting hungry in breadlines?
4. Why did the Hoover administration seem paralyzed in providing basic essentials like food?
5. Considering the Bonus March later in 1932, was that year perhaps the lowest point in the Great Depression?

Document 4.2. Franklin D. Roosevelt's Inaugural Address

As this chapter makes clear, FDR was preparing to do political battle with Hoover in the 1932 presidential election. Roosevelt, as governor of our largest state, had experimented with a series of New Deal initiatives in New York. After securing the Democratic Party nomination, Franklin Roosevelt and his Brain Trust of advisers prepared to unveil his far-reaching innovative efforts. Winning in the November 1932 election, Roosevelt took office in March 1933, wasting little time as he implemented a fundamental change in direction for the federal government during the Hundred Days, as described in this chapter. Below is a brief passage from the new president's inaugural address.

> So first of all let me assert my firm belief that the only thing we have to fear is fear itself—nameless, unreasoning, unjustified terror which paralyzes needed efforts to convert retreat into advance.

Thinking Historically

1. Did Franklin Roosevelt believe that the electorate and Congress would rally around his New Deal?
2. Is the new president correct in identifying "fear" as America's enemy in 1933?
3. Is the Hundred Days a useful yardstick for measuring his plan to rescue our capitalist system?
4. Why did this flurry of initial initiatives not solve the Great Depression?
5. Was FDR's plan radical or reassuring to the citizens?

Document 4.3. Roosevelt's "Quarantine" Speech

Encountering America's traditional isolationism and the voices of foreign policy critics who were wary of a second world war, Franklin Roosevelt used a 1937 speech in Chicago to alert our citizens to the threat posed by totalitarian dictators like Hitler, Mussolini, and the Japanese military, all of which by that year had demonstrated their aggressive intentions. The following is an excerpt from the commander in chief's "Quarantine" speech.

> The political situation in the world, which of late has been growing progressively worse, as such as to cause grave concern and anxiety to all the peoples and nations who wish to live in peace and amity with their neighbors. ...
> America hates war. America hopes for peace. Therefore, America actively engages in the search for peace.

Thinking Historically

1. Who were the audiences that Roosevelt was trying to influence with his remarks?
2. Was he, in 1937, trying to unite the world's democratic nations, America included, in a common cause?
3. Why did the totalitarian nations of the world ignore FDR's call for a "quarantine" of aggressors?
4. Even though the president was coming off another electoral victory, why did Congress and organizations such as America First hold fast to neutrality?
5. How successful was the chief executive in "educating" the American people about the threat posed by the dictatorships?

Document 4.4. Nesei Internment

The surprise attack at Pearl Harbor on December 7, 1941, unleashed hatred for Japan. That Christmas, Roosevelt entertained Great Britain's prime minister at the White House. The president sought the advice of elected officials like California governor Earl Warren and Federal Bureau of Investigation director J. Edgar Hoover about the threat of Japanese espionage on our shores. Warren urged the detention of Nisei, second-generation Japanese Americans, as a proper response to the Japanese actions in the Pacific Theater. Hoover, on the other hand, stressed that the Nisei were loyal Americans. As we have learned, mistreatment of minority populations is a theme in our nation's history. Roosevelt took the advice of Warren and forced the Nisei to sell their businesses and homes and be placed in detention camps. The Supreme Court backed FDR, and it was not until the presidency of Ronald Reagan in 1988 that an apology was issued and compensation of $20,000 paid to each of the 62,000 survivors. The following is an excerpt from President Roosevelt's 1942 executive order on the subject.

Whereas the successful prosecution of the war requires every possible protection against espionage and against sabotage to national-defense material, national-defense premises, and national-defense utilities.

Thinking Historically

1. What do this detention order and the Supreme Court's endorsement of it tell us about a commander in chief's powers in times of war?
2. Since we were also at war with Nazi Germany and fascist Italy by early 1942, why were their populations in America not considered "espionage" and "sabotage" threats?
3. What role did race play in Roosevelt's actions against the Nisei?
4. Why did the attack at Pearl Harbor mobilize public support of FDR's executive order?
5. Why did it take over forty years for this presidential action to be revisited?

Document 4.5. Maps of Europe and Asia, World War II

After the attack at Pearl Harbor, we found ourselves allied with Great Britain, the Free French who resisted Hitler, and communist Stalin of the Soviet Union. The war became for the United States initially a war against the Japanese in the Pacific Theater while Stalin urged an attack against the Nazis who were pummeling his country. As this chapter explains, Stalin wanted a Second Front launched in Nazi-held France to relieve Nazi pressure on the Soviet Union, but that invasion did not occur until D-Day in 1944 as this chapter notes. By that time, American forces were assisting Italian partisans who were pursuing Mussolini's fascists. Additionally, Americans were battling Nazis in North Africa. These composite maps illustrate that World War II had become a truly global conflict for America.

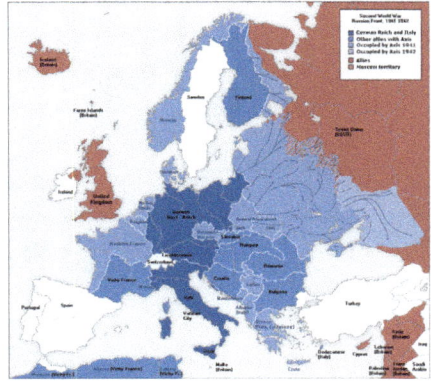

IMG 4.1a: Copyright © by ArmadniGeneral (CC BY-SA 3.0) at https://commons.wikimedia.org/wiki/File:Second_world_war_europe_1941-1942_map_en.png.

IMG 4.1b: Source: https://www.loc.gov/resource/g7400.ct002001/

Thinking Historically

1. How difficult was it for Roosevelt and the allied commanders to maintain unity in the war?
2. Were behind-the-lines groups like the Free French and the Italian partisans essential to ultimate victory?
3. Why was American General Dwight Eisenhower the ideal choice to lead the allied forces at D-Day?
4. Did the 1919 Paris Peace Conference make this more deadly war inevitable?
5. How did the slowness in opening the Second Front lay the groundwork for the Cold War?

5

CONTAINMENT

President Truman was convinced that his use of atomic bombs hastened the end of World War II, saving American and Japanese lives. The devastation of Hiroshima and Nagasaki was immense and sent a clear message that the United States possessed deadly new weapons. Within a few weeks of Japan's September 1945 surrender, our military forces returned home, and the baby boom began. Families were reunited and children were born into a new, dangerous world. The alliance with Joseph Stalin's Soviet Union, a totalitarian state with a communist command economy, ended and a Cold War commenced. This conflict would produce tensions between our two nations until the Soviet Union detonated its own atomic weapons in 1949, holding the nuclear advantage. The world became bipolar—"us versus them"—and it would witness rivalry in Europe, Asia, Africa, and the Middle East. Western democracies rallied around the United States, while conquered lands fell to Stalin. Perhaps the use of atomic bombs in the summer of 1945 was intended to send a clear message to "them": we possessed the willingness to defend our friends.

Prime Minister Winston Churchill was defeated for reelection in the United Kingdom that summer. In 1946, he visited the United States, receiving an honorary degree from Missouri's Westminster College and speaking of an "Iron Curtain" that had descended on the communist world (see Document 5.1). Truman demonstrated his commitment to spending huge amounts of resources to contain communism. He feared that war-torn nations were susceptible to communist ideology. The first test of this commitment took place in 1947 in Greece and Turkey. Under the Truman Doctrine, the government spent $400,000,000 to prevent the communist expansion of the iron curtain to those two nations.

Secretary of State George C. Marshall later that year articulated an even larger aid program that would help rebuild Europe and prevent it from becoming a satellite of Stalin. This Marshall Plan amounted to billions of dollars in economic credits to prevent Europe from becoming communist. State Department aide George F. Kennan spelled out the rationale of containment: a long, sustained, expensive effort was required to block communist expansion. Our two systems were locked in a protracted rivalry, and we must be vigilant, Kennan argued.

Truman secured victory in the 1948 presidential election, vigorously campaigning against Republican Thomas Dewey, former FDR vice president Henry Wallace (who favored a more conciliatory approach to the Soviet Union), and Dixiecrat Strom Thurmond who criticized Truman's pro-civil rights program (including integration of the military) and his domestic Fair Deal. Within months, however, the news came from Moscow that the Soviets now had their own atomic bomb. Additionally, in 1949, the communists under Mao Zedong ousted Chiang Kai-shek from the mainland of China, sending him into exile on the island of Taiwan. The question being asked became, "Who lost China?" Americans became uneasy about the Cold War.

One of Roosevelt's goals had been the establishment of a United Nations (UN) organization where nations would talk and negotiate instead of fight. While FDR did not live long enough to see the actual formation of the UN, it would be tested by the end of the 1940s as the Americans and Soviets, both members of the new organization's Security Council, maneuvered for supremacy.

The Soviets had secured their own nuclear arsenal with the help of communist sympathizers in our government, such as Julius and Ethel Rosenberg who were executed as spies in 1950. One target became Alger Hiss, an aide to Roosevelt who was defended by Truman. In congressional hearings in 1948 and 1949, California representative Richard Nixon questioned Hiss's loyalties, and Hiss would be imprisoned for perjury.

US senator Joseph McCarthy took his search for "reds" in our government a step further (see Document 5.2). In a 1950 Wheeling, West Virginia, radio address, the Wisconsin senator alleged that there were numerous communists in our state department. The Red Scare had begun, and the Truman administration seemed to not take questions of loyalty among our government officials seriously. One senator, Maine's Margaret Chase Smith, resisted McCarthy's tactics (see Document 5.3). She raised questions about her fellow senator's bullying of anyone he deemed disloyal.

In 1950, Truman's new secretary of state, Dean Acheson, told an interviewer that there were some places on earth where we would militarily confront communist aggression: Japan and the Philippines, for example. But Korea was not a priority. The communist interpreted this statement as a green light to attack noncommunist South Korea. While it was a nondeclared war, merely a "police action," the Korean conflict tested the UN. With the Soviets boycotting the organization because of the nonadmittance of Communist China, the UN responded with a bloody war, which was commanded by our general Douglas MacArthur, ultimately costing 33,000 American lives and $22,000,000,000 on that faraway peninsula. Containment now cost lives as well as treasure.

This police action, occurring so soon after the end of World War II, created anxiety and division. Truman fired MacArthur in 1951 for risking a larger conflict as the result of the general's refusal to reestablish the border between North and South Korea at the 38th parallel, recklessly risking a nuclear war with Mao's China (see Document 5.4). The conflict ended in 1953 with a tense armistice, as well as the inauguration of a new president, General Dwight Eisenhower, who vowed to contain communism ("I will go to Korea," Eisenhower pledged in his campaign). As the architect of 1944's D-Day invasion,

Eisenhower understood the human and financial cost of war, and he was determined to resist the temptation of a nuclear clash with the Soviet Union and China. The world that Eisenhower inherited in 1953 was fraught with danger. The Cold War had proven itself to be exceedingly hot for many Americans as the world separated into spheres of influence between the United States and the Soviet Union (see Document 5.5). "Ike," as he was affectionately called, would also inherit a nation dealing with barriers—racial, cultural, military, and atmospheric.

Document 5.1. Winston Churchill's "Iron Curtain" Speech, 1946

Winston Churchill's relationship with FDR went back to the Great War, even though FDR seemed unclear about that initial meeting. Both men had been on the political stage for decades. Before Pearl Harbor, they conferred off the coast of Canada and issued the Atlantic Charter, a statement of solidarity among the United States and the United Kingdom as Churchill resisted the Nazis. Despite American neutrality, Roosevelt pushed through Congress measures of assistance, as this chapter mentions (e.g., bases for destroyers, lend lease). When December 7, 1941, occurred, the two leaders and Stalin frequently met to discuss the war's developments. At the last conference in February 1945, the Big Three met in the Soviet city of Yalta, with an ill Roosevelt trying to hold the alliance together. After FDR's death, Truman, Stalin, and Churchill met at Potsdam to chart the war's end. Ironically, Great Britain's electorate defeated Churchill during the summer of 1945, and Churchill stepped aside as prime minister. By early 1946, he visited the United States, speaking at Westminster College in Fulton, Missouri, warning of a new threat to democracy, originating in Moscow. The following excerpt is a portion of Churchill's iron curtain remarks.

> A shadow has fallen upon the scenes so lately lighted by the Allied victory. Nobody knows what Soviet Russia and its Communist international organization (*sic*) intends to do in the immediate future, or what are the limits, if any, to their expansive and proselytizing tendencies. ...
>
> From Stettin in the Baltic to Trieste in the Adriatic, an iron curtain has descended across the continent.

Thinking Historically

1. Analyze the causes of the Cold War, which split the alliance between the Western democracies and Stalin's Soviet Union.
2. Was Churchill correct about Soviet ambitions?
3. Why did the former prime minister's comments alarm the West, especially the United States?
4. Could Churchill be considered the architect of containment?
5. How did the Truman administration respond to the lowering of the iron curtain?

Document 5.2. Senator McCarthy's Radio Address, 1950

By 1950, the Soviets had detonated their own atomic bomb and China had become communist. The world had become a much more dangerous place. Wisconsin senator Joseph McCarthy sounded the alarm that communists had infiltrated the Truman Administration, specifically the state department. The Red Scare was underway, and McCarthy was urging that saboteurs in our own government were hard at work undermining our democracy. Truman rejected this premise, but many Americans took McCarthy's warning seriously. The following is a portion of McCarthy's 1950 radio speech in Wheeling, West Virginia. Historians disagree on the number of communists the senator cited: 205, 81, 57, or "a lot."

> The reason why we find ourselves in a position of impotency is not because our only powerful potential enemy has sent men to invade our shores, but rather because of the traitorous actions of those who have been treated so well by this Nation. It has not been the less fortunate or members of minority groups who have been selling this Nation out, but rather those who have had all the benefits that the wealthiest nation on earth has had to offer—the finest homes, the finest college education, and the finest jobs in Government we can give.

Thinking Historically

1. Discuss the logic of Senator McCarthy's 1950 radio warning.
2. Did President Truman's rejection of McCarthy's claims make matters worse?
3. Considering the status of the Cold War and containment in 1950, did events give credibility to McCarthy's allegations?
4. Did the eruption of war on the Korean Peninsula that year create an audience of supporters for McCarthy?
5. How should we evaluate McCarthy and his warning in the modern era?

Document 5.3. "Declaration of Conscience"

As this chapter mentions, few national figures were willing to resist Joseph McCarthy's Red Scare. One was Maine Senator Margaret Chase Smith who answered by saying that she spoke as a fellow Republican, a woman, a senator, and an American. Her 1950 response, excerpted next, is called "Declaration of Conscience." She criticized her fellow legislators, the Truman administration, and loyalty commissions. Interestingly, the Senate censured McCarthy in 1954 for questioning the loyalty of our military during televised hearings.

> I would like to speak briefly and simply about a serious national condition. It is a national feeling of fear and frustration that could result in national

suicide and the end of everything that we Americans hold dear. It is a condition that comes from the lack of effective leadership in either the Legislative Branch or the Executive Branch of our Government.

That leadership is so lacking that serious and responsible proposals are being made that national advisory commissions be appointed to provide such critically needed leadership.

Thinking Historically

1. Why is Senator Smith one of the few voices being raised in 1950 to object to what she labeled "national suicide"?
2. In Cold War America, was Smith accurately identifying the "threat" to our democracy?
3. Was McCarthy perhaps the real challenge to liberty?
4. What does his 1954 censure by his fellow senators tell us about the recklessness of McCarthy's approach?
5. How do you assess Smith's "Declaration of Conscience"?

Document 5.4. Truman Fires General MacArthur

Since the Korean "police action" was a UN effort, it had a clear goal upon which that international body agreed: the reestablishment of the border between communist Korea and democratic South Korea. As the war proceeded, General Douglas MacArthur accomplished that goal by 1951, but he proceeded into North Korea, despite warnings from President Truman. The general advocated air strikes against communist China, which was supplying the North Koreans, and risked overt involvement by the Soviets. As commander in chief, Truman, fearful of losing UN's support and igniting a nuclear war, fired MacArthur. This action divided our nation but demonstrated the importance of civilian control of our military. Here is an excerpt of Truman's remarks on the subject.

> I believe that we must try to limit the war to Korea for these vital reasons: To make sure that the precious lives of our fighting men are not wasted, to see that the security of our country and the free world is not needlessly jeopardized, and to prevent a third world war.
>
> A number of events have made it evident that General MacArthur did not agree with that policy. I have, therefore, considered it essential to relieve General MacArthur so that there would be no doubt or confusion as to the real purpose and aim of our policy.

Thinking Historically

1. Was General MacArthur justified in pursuing the communist forces beyond the 38th Parallel, which divided North and South Korea?

2. Years earlier, President Roosevelt called MacArthur one of the most dangerous men in America. Does this 1951 clash with Truman explain that characterization?
3. The Founding Fathers in the Constitution gave the president ultimate control of our military. Why?
4. Why did many Americans favor MacArthur's approach in Korea?
5. How do you evaluate Truman's firing of the military commander?

Document 5.5. Map of the Cold War

By 1950, the world was divided between us and them, as this chapter makes clear. Democratic and communist nations kept a watchful eye trained on one another, as well as their respective nuclear arsenals. It was only five years since World War II ended, but we were immersed in a Cold War, which, as we saw in this chapter, became boiling hot in Korea. The following map illustrates this bipolar world as the United States sought to contain communist advancement.

IMG 5.1: Copyright © 1950 by Robert M. Chapin. Source: https://digital.library.cornell.edu/catalog/ss:3293969.

Thinking Historically

1. The Soviet Union had a historical fear of "encirclement." Was this fear justified?
2. What geographic, cultural, social, and political values united the Western nations?
3. As you look at the non-Western nations of the Middle East, Africa, Asia, and Latin America, why would they figure into the Cold War?
4. Were we winning the Cold War in the 1950s?
5. Why would the following three decades prove to be a continuation of the conflict between "us and them"?

6

BARRIERS

The deal that gave a narrow one-vote electoral college victory to Republican Rutherford B. Hayes after the 1876 presidential election required all Union troops still occupying the South to be withdrawn. Their presence had shielded African Americans from abuse by terrorists like the Ku Klux Klan. Howard University philosophy professor Alain Locke labeled the result "the nadir of the Negro." Without the support of the military, ex-slaves, indeed, entered the twilight. Racial barriers replaced the deployed troops, and segregation separated the races in what would be called the Jim Crow Era, a time when lynchings occurred throughout the South, as well as discrimination and disenfranchisement.

In 1896, the US Supreme Court endorsed this inequality. The case *Plessy v. Ferguson* focused on seating arrangements on Louisiana railroad cars. Homer Plessy sued the state because he was seven-eighths White and confined to cars for Blacks. Under state law, Plessy had to sit in a car reserved for African Americans. The justices issued a landmark decision that went far beyond Louisiana and railroad transportation. The court ruled that "separate but equal" was now the guiding principle. Unfortunately, the "equal" part of that mandate would be ignored, but the "separate" part became rigidly enforced across the land regarding transportation, accommodations, dining, education, medical services, and entertainment.

By Woodrow Wilson's presidency, his southern bias was evident when he called the racist 1915 movie *The Birth of a Nation*, with its glorification of the Old South and the Ku Klux Klan, "history written with lightning." Wilson grew up in Columbia, South Carolina, and as a child witnessed Confederate general Robert E. Lee visit the city after the Civil War. When he became president, Wilson separated federal employees on the basis of race.

Even though First Lady Eleanor Roosevelt sought the advice of leaders in the African American community and tried to make sure they were not ignored by New Deal programs, her husband was cautious on the issue of civil rights, not wishing to upset powerful southern members of Congress. It would be FDR's successor, Harry Truman who integrated the military in 1948 and pursued civil rights measures in fair employment. Unfortunately, racial segregation remained during the Eisenhower administration.

In 1954, the barriers shook when the Supreme Court, in the *Brown v. Board of Education* decision, overturned the 1896 *Plessy* ruling. This case, a collection of cases from Kansas, South Carolina, Virginia, and Delaware, focused on segregated schools and the damage that such schools did to African American students. The NAACP Legal Defense Fund brought in psychologists Kenneth and Mamie Clark who demonstrated that segregated schools were affecting self-esteem among African Americans at an early age. The court's justices agreed and ruled that "separate but equal schools were inherently unequal" (see Document 6.1).

The *Brown* decision omitted a time frame for when this educational imbalance in instruction, facilities, and teacher salaries should end. In 1955, the court added "with all deliberate speed." It would be years, however, before the court-ordered immediate correction of the situation. Removal of discriminatory barriers was a slow process, and it could be violent.

While on a visit to his relatives in Money, Mississippi, in 1955, 15-year-old Emmett Till fell victim to that violence. Till, from Chicago, committed an affront to two White women. What was said was undoubtedly insignificant. But the husband of one of the White women and a group of White men visited the home where Till was staying and told Till's uncle, "We want the boy that did all that talking." Kidnapping the teenager, the Whites beat him to death and tied the body to a concrete flywheel, throwing Till into the water. When the lifeless body was retrieved, Till's mother insisted that an open casket be used at his services, with his battered face appearing in publications such as *Jet* magazine, which was distributed around the nation.

In nearby Alabama, the Montgomery Improvement Association (MIA) took aim at that city's segregated municipal bus system. NAACP member Rosa Parks refused to give up her seat on a bus to a White passenger, a planned protest that launched a year-long boycott of the city's transportation by African American patrons. Led by Rev. Dr. Martin Luther King Jr. and others, the MIA rallied the city's African American population, using carpools to get citizens to their jobs. By late 1956, the city of Montgomery, losing revenue, agreed to integrate municipal barriers.

Dr. King and his allies formed the Southern Christian Leadership Conference in 1957, an organization that practiced nonviolence, used a network of churches, and used his ministerial and media skills to draw public attention to the racial barriers in the South. That same year, President Eisenhower used the military to integrate Central High School in Arkansas (see Document 6.2). For a year, soldiers escorted nine African American students past jeering Whites, safely removing the educational barriers at Central High.

By the mid-1950s, other barriers were being challenged. In Tupelo, Mississippi, Elvis Presley unleashed his brand of music, learned at African American clubs, on society. He gyrated, sneered, and sang "Blue Suede Shoes," "Nothing But a Hound Dog," "Are You Lonesome Tonight?," and "Heartbreak Hotel." When he appeared on the popular *Ed Sullivan Show*, female television audiences shrieked in ecstasy, even though parents frowned at what would be called "Rock and Roll." At America's movies in the 1950s, Marilyn Monroe thrilled male viewers in a string of titillating films: *The Seven Year Itch*, *Bus Stop*, and *Gentlemen Prefer Blonds*.

On television, game shows like *The $64,000 Question* and *Twenty-One* became popular. The latter toppled *The Lucy Show* from atop the ratings; however, in 1956, it was revealed that it had been rigged by producers.

During the decade's last years, conflict occurred in the Middle East between Israel and its Muslim neighbors, and the Cold War was unabated. In 1957, special ambassador James P. Richards explained the Eisenhower Doctrine to that strategic oil-rich region's leaders (see Document 6.3). Richards dispensed $200,000,000 in economic and military assistance to those who stood with the United States against "international communism." Oil and our recognition in 1948 of the modern state of Israel (at the cost of Palestine) increased our interest in the Middle East.

In 1957, the Soviet Union launched the planet's first satellite, *Sputnik* (Traveler). Soviet premier Nikita Khrushchev proclaimed, "*Sputnik* is getting lonely up there," ridiculing our failed attempt to send our own "traveler" aloft. The space race began as we followed in 1958 with our own successful effort. The Soviets then sent a dog into space, and we followed with a chimpanzee. The earth's atmosphere had been pierced as outer space was removed as a barrier. In the 1960s, the competition continued with human cargo.

Students enrolled at North Carolina A&T, a historically black institution in Greensboro, North Carolina, challenged segregated lunch counters in 1960. These "sit-in" civil rights protests became front-page stories (Document 6.4) and demonstrated to the world the societal barriers that even extended to lunch counters where African Americans could not eat a snack beside Whites. The following year in South Carolina, nine college students, the Friendship (College) Nine, similarly protested. The difference was that these young men refused to post bail. The new civil rights strategy would be "jail no bail." The country paid close attention to these protests, as well as those of Dr. King.

The changing of the guard was about to occur at the White House. Ike was about to step aside after winning two terms as president. A new youthful president, Massachusetts's John F. Kennedy (JFK) was about to be inaugurated. Before he left office in January 1961, however, Eisenhower, the hero of D-Day who had spent much of his life in uniform, issued a stern warning about the powerful growth of the military-industrial complex and the cozy relationship between weapons' manufacturers and the political establishment (see Document 6.5). He feared that in a world with nuclear weapons, we could find ourselves facing Armageddon, stumbling into another world war.

Document 6.1. *Brown v. Board of Education*

As this anthology makes clear, one of the themes of our nation's history is the denial of human rights to certain ethnic groups. In 1896, the Supreme Court ruled in the *Plessy* decision that "separate but equal" was the law of the land, thus erecting racial barriers. By 1954, however, a collection of cases challenged substandard education in Kansas, South Carolina, Virginia, and Delaware. With the assistance of the NAACP Legal Defense

Fund and sociologists, *Brown v. Board of Education* unanimously overturned the earlier ruling. The following is an excerpt from that mandate.

> We conclude that in the field of public education the doctrine of "separate but equal" has no place. Separate educational facilities are inherently unequal. Therefore, we hold that the plaintiffs and others similarly situated for whom the actions have been brought are, by reason of the segregation complained of, deprived of the equal protection of the laws guaranteed by the Fourteenth Amendment.

Thinking Historically

1. Why is it significant that this decision was a unanimous nine to zero?
2. What, exactly, does "equal protection of the laws" mean?
3. After 1954, many southern states delayed implementing integration. Why?
4. Resistance to this landmark ruling took the form of the creation of White citizens councils in some states. What was their goal?
5. Complete school integration did not occur until 1970, 16 years after *Brown*. Explain why.

Document 6.2. Dwight D. Eisenhower's Radio Address, 1957

In the fall of 1957, President Eisenhower sent federal troops to Little Rock, Arkansas, to protect nine African American students who were trying to integrate Central High School. Eisenhower backed a federal court, which had decided in favor of these students. Violence and jeering crowds had impeded the students, and the president addressed the nation on September 24, 1957. Here is a portion of those radio remarks.

> And so, with deep confidence, I call upon citizens of the State of Arkansas to assist in bringing an immediate end to all interference with the law and its processes. If resistance to the Federal Court order ceases at once, the further presence of Federal troops will be unnecessary and the city of Little Rock will return to its normal habits of peace and order—and a blot upon the fair name and high honor of our nation will be removed.
>
> Thus will be restored the image of America and of its parts as one nation, indivisible, with liberty and justice for all.

Thinking Historically

1. Why did communist nations criticize the events occurring in Little Rock?
2. Federal troops had not been used in the South since 1877. Why is this action by the president significant?
3. Why did Arkansas governor Orval Faubus object?

4. What authority did the president have for his decision?
5. What does the fact that federal troops had to remain at Central High for eight months tell us?

Document 6.3. The Eisenhower Doctrine

As the Cold War raged, the Eisenhower administration worried about communist encroachment in the oil-rich Middle East. In 1957, the president, with congressional support, issued the Eisenhower Doctrine. A former member of Congress, James P. Richards, was appointed to visit the region and dispense $200,000,000 in military and economic assistance to countries that stated their opposition to "international communism" in the strategic area. In three months, Ambassador Richards visited 15 nations, traveling 30,000 miles. Here is a portion of this Cold War measure.

> If the president determines the necessity thereof, the United States is prepared to use armed force to assist any such nation or group of nations requesting assistance against armed aggression from any country controlled by international communism.

Thinking Historically

1. What role did America's support in the 1948 creation of the modern state of Israel play in this diplomatic effort?
2. Define "international communism."
3. Compare this initiative with the earlier Truman Doctrine.
4. Why was the Middle East so crucial to American foreign policy?
5. Why did Ambassador Richards encounter only lukewarm support in some nations, such as Afghanistan and Yemen, and fail to meet with the leaders of Egypt and Jordan?

Document 6.4. Civil Rights Protests in 1960

As this chapter explains, by 1960, civil rights protesters had new weapons at their disposal. Often, college students were on the front lines of these protests. That was true in Greensboro, North Carolina, home of North Carolina A&T, an African American institution. Angry that they could not be served at a Woolworth's lunch counter, in February 1960, students sat at the so-called dime store's counter anyway, getting arrested and gaining national media coverage of their action. Here is part of an editorial from that city's newspaper.

This is a problem for Greensboro's mayor or city manager, working on the one hand with the Woolworth management, and responsible Negro leadership on the other.

There is a proper way to handle such matters, and it ought be resorted to before something much more serious happens at the five and ten.

Thinking Historically

1. Why do the college sit-in protests focus attention so effectively on the prevalence of racial barriers?
2. What point does the Greensboro newspaper miss in its 1960 editorial?
3. Why did young protesters such as the North Carolina A&T students find themselves on the front lines?
4. Why did discrimination such as this persist into the new decade of the 1960s?
5. How did the 1961 "jail no bail" protest in South Carolina by Friendship College students intensify the civil rights movement?

Document 6.5. Eisenhower's Farewell Address

As he approached retirement, President Eisenhower issued his farewell address, a warning about the nuclear weapons being amassed by both sides in the Cold War and the close relationship between arms manufacturers and our government. The former general had witnessed war close up and knew the risks posed by the twentieth century's weapons of mass destruction. His speech, excerpted next, was a plea for sanity and restraint.

> As one who has witnessed the horror and the lingering sadness of war—as one who knows that another war could utterly destroy this civilization which has been slowly and painfully built over thousands of years—I wish I could say tonight that a lasting peace is in sight.
>
> Happily, I can say that war has been avoided. Steady progress toward our ultimate goal has been made. But, so much remains to be done. As a private citizen, I shall never cease to do what little I can to help the world advance along that road.

Thinking Historically

1. Is President Eisenhower's farewell address optimistic or pessimistic about the prospects for world peace?
2. Place this speech into the larger context of the Cold War.
3. Does the fact that he is a former military leader give Eisenhower's plea added weight?
4. What, exactly, does Eisenhower fear in the 1960s?
5. Why was his cautionary advice largely ignored?

7

NEW FRONTIERS

The tensions of the 1950s overflowed into the 1960s. Throughout the Eisenhower years, the battle against communist expansion was unrelenting. In 1953, the Central Intelligence Agency (CIA) was vigilant, always looking for the Red Tide, which seemed to be spreading. Moving quickly that year, the agency supported an effort to reinstall a friendly government in Iran, which occupied a strategic base for watching the neighboring Soviet Union. The shah of Iran was a pliable ally, not popular among his own people but popular in Washington. Similarly, the CIA supported a dependable ally in Guatemala in 1954. Closer was Cuba, where American business interests, some with organized crime ties, and a dictator, Fulgencio Batista, were in control. As long as Batista was anti-communist, the Eisenhower administration tolerated his graft and abuse of his people.

By 1959, Cuba revolutionary Fidel Castro was fighting Batista forces. Eisenhower was assured that Castro was not a friend of Moscow. His popularity among the Cuban public, long abused by the Batista regime, was undeniable. The country was dominated by American mobsters and Batista's cronies. Thus, Eisenhower withdrew his support of Batista, who fled with his fortune. Almost immediately, Castro announced to a cheering Havana crowd that he was indeed a Marxist. This embarrassment consumed the last year of the Eisenhower term as the CIA planned an invasion by American-trained Cuban exiles to topple the communists in our hemisphere. Time ran out to launch the invasion, however, and the Castro problem would be inherited by the next administration.

The Eisenhower administration was further embarrassed in its last year when a spy plane, the U-2, was shot down over the Soviet Union. Our president denied the incident, but Soviet premier Nikita Khrushchev promptly paraded around the CIA pilot, Francis Gary Powers, whom our government thought had committed suicide as the U-2 plane was targeted. A 1960 summit meeting between the United States and the Soviet Union became a casualty of the downing of the spy plane.

In Southeast Asia, communist forces led by Ho Chi Minh, who had worked with the Americans during the last days of World War II against the Japanese, had defeated the French at Dien Bien Phu in 1954. Eisenhower had resisted coming to the aid of France by supplying American ground forces or nuclear weapons. Millions of dollars had been spent, however, by both Truman and Eisenhower to bolster France in its losing effort to cling to its Asian colonial empire. This region would, also, be a trouble spot for the new American president, JFK.

The Massachusetts senator was a decorated World War II hero, surviving the sinking of his patrol boat by the Japanese in 1943. His wealthy father had publicized the incident, and Kennedy returned home to win a seat in the House of Representatives in 1946. Advancing to the Senate in 1952, JFK, with support from the large Kennedy family, as well as Joseph P. Kennedy's fortune, aimed higher. In 1956, Kennedy nearly secured the Democratic Party's vice-presidential nomination. Almost immediately, Kennedy began planning a 1960 White House bid.

Kennedy's Catholicism was an issue that year, but his father's associates and the campaigning family were able to win the party's presidential nomination. Helping was JFK's vivacious young wife, Jackie, and young daughter, Caroline. The Kennedys were full of vigor and grace and connections. The country awaited in January 1961 for what JFK had called the New Frontier. Swept away would be the aging Eisenhower, as well as Vice President Richard Nixon, who had narrowly lost the November 1960 election. "New" was an appropriate adjective for what was about to occur in America.

After eight inches of new snow had fallen overnight in the nation's capital, JFK took the oath of office. He spoke of "the torch of leadership being passed to a new generation." He vowed that America would "go anywhere, bear any burden in defense of liberty." Our citizens should look for ways to serve the nation, the 43-year-old president urged (see Document 7.1). The New Frontier had been born on a frosty January 20, 1961, as the old leadership watched, shivering in the Washington cold. But the Cold War was still blazing, and Cuba emerged as a challenge.

The establishment of a communist foothold in the Caribbean angered and embarrassed the Eisenhower administration, but time ran out, and the Castro problem was handed off to Kennedy. Exiles were trained and poised to topple Castro if the new president approved. The CIA emphasized the likely success of such an effort, but JFK wanted to ensure that America's role was minimal. Finally, on April 7, 1961, the American surrogates headed from Nicaragua to the Bay of Pigs. It became a fiasco within 48 hours. Castro seemed to know the invaders were coming; word had leaked. The Cuban people themselves seemed satisfied with the communists. The Bay of Pigs had coral reefs that damaged the exiles' boats. Exasperated, Kennedy refused to provide more than minimal air support. Watching all this from Moscow was Castro's patron, Nikita Khrushchev. Admirably, JFK took total responsibility for the failure. Cuba would take center stage again the following year.

The decade's New Frontiers extended into outer space. The Eisenhower administration had established the National Aeronautics and Space Administration (NASA) in 1958 as a response to the Soviet Union's launch of *Sputnik*. One month after the debacle in Cuba, the United States sent astronaut Alan Shepard into space, In May 1961, the new president vowed to send astronauts to the moon by the end of the decade. He told Congress that "landing a man on the Moon and returning him safely to Earth" would demonstrate America's technological prowess. It would, also, send a clear message to the communists, as would Kennedy's Peace Corps of idealistic Americans fanning out around the world.

The message that Khrushchev had for Kennedy was delivered at a two-day meeting in Vienna in early June. The Soviet leader lambasted the Americans for the Bay of Pigs fiasco. He sized up JFK as young, inexperienced, and weak. Tensions were escalating in Berlin, which had been a focal point in the Truman years because it was located deep in communist East Germany and precariously divided between the Soviets, French, British, and Americans. There was a brain drain of talented East Berliners fleeing to the West that summer. Khrushchev's response in August 1961 was the erection of the Berlin Wall, a barrier between free and communist parts of that city.

As 1962 began, Americans continued to reach skyward. In February, astronaut John Glenn orbited the earth three times. He was followed in May by Scott Carpenter, and in early October Walter Schirra circled the globe six times. Those achievements were supplemented by the publication that year of two significant books: Michael Harrington's *The Other America* and Rachel Carson's *Silent Spring*. The former work examined poverty in our country, and the latter sounded the alarm about environmental pollution. Readers and policy makers became more aware of the challenges facing this earth.

The Cold War continued. American troops were placed in the Southeast Asian nation of Laos in May 1962, "a diplomatic solution" to communist encroachment, Kennedy called it. It would be Cuba, however, which would pose a much larger problem that year. American surveillance planes spotted nuclear weapons' facilities on the island. The Soviets initially lied about their intentions, but photographs taken by the U-2 planes substantiated that the weapons were indeed there. On October 22, 1962, JFK announced a "quarantine" of the communist island. The world seemed poised for a nuclear holocaust. Miraculously, an accommodation was reached: the Soviets removed the offensive nuclear weapons; we removed missiles from Turkey which bordered the Soviet Union, and we privately pledged not to attempt to topple Fidel Castro again (see Documents 7.2 and 7.3).

The racial barriers in education continued to be pierced in 1962. The University of Alabama accepted its first African American student, despite the resistance of the state's segregationist governor, George Wallace, who stood in the doorway. Integration of the University of Mississippi would come with violence and military presence the following year. Dr. King wrote an impassioned letter in the spring of 1963 while he sat in a Birmingham jail. He criticized White "moderate" ministers who were timidly unwilling to join his effort to provide justice to people of color. In August 1963, King spoke to 250,000 Americans assembled in Washington. He stood on the steps of the Lincoln Memorial and told the multiracial crowd about his "dream" of a United States where color would not separate us.

Kennedy continued to be focused on the communists of Southeast Asia, Vietnam to be specific. Slowly, our troop presence, "advisers," increased. On November 1, 1963, the leader of South Vietnam, President Diem, was assassinated with American complicity because he was deemed ineffective in the clash with communists. By the end of that month, Kennedy himself had been killed during a November 22 visit to Dallas, Texas.

The 1964 Warren Commission blamed Lee Harvey Oswald for the murder of JFK. The nation wept as his young widow, Jackie, and his two children led the country through an emotional farewell burial ceremony atop Arlington's cemetery. Later, Jackie Kennedy would call the 1,000 days of the Kennedy presidency "Camelot," a sparkling time when the men were knights, and the women were fair maidens.

It would be Vice President Lyndon B. Johnson (LBJ) who would inherit the bloodied remnants of the New Frontier. He was a Texan, experienced in the ways of Washington by his earlier service in the US Senate, and he would prove masterful at shoving through Congress the 1964 Civil Rights Act. Where Kennedy had been cautious in antagonizing powerful southern members of Congress, Johnson seemed to relish the clash. By August 1964, LBJ was proclaiming a war on poverty, a Great Society he labeled it (Document 7.4). It was a noble experiment, and the Democratic Party seemed to rally to Johnson's dream (Document 7.5). It would be another type of "war," the one in Southeast Asia, which would prove divisive as the United States embarked on a perilous roller-coaster ride.

Document 7.1. John F. Kennedy's Inaugural Address

As the youngest elected president, 43-year-old JFK began the New Frontier with soaring rhetoric on inauguration day, January 20, 1961. His 1,000-day presidency would be called by his widow, Jackie Kennedy, "Camelot," a mystical time of vigor and challenges. In his inaugural address on a frosty day, complete with the poetry of octogenarian Robert Frost, Kennedy spoke of "the torch of leadership" being passed from the old generation to a youthful one, born in the twentieth century. He urged America to "ask not what your country can do for you but what you can do for your country." We Americans "would go anywhere" in the defense of liberty. The following is an excerpt from that memorable speech.

> The world is very different now. For man holds in his mortal hands the power to abolish all forms of human poverty and all forms of human life. And yet the same revolutionary beliefs for which our forebears fought are still at issue around the globe—the belief that the rights of man come not from the generosity of the state but from the hand of God.
>
> We dare not forget today that we are the heirs of that first revolution. Let the word go forth from this time and place, to friend and foe alike, that the torch of leadership has been passed to a new generation of Americans—born in this century, tempered by war, disciplined by a hard and bitter peace, proud of our ancient heritage.

Thinking Historically

1. What is the tone John Kennedy is trying to convey for this "new" generation of American leadership?

2. How is this tone different from the aged Dwight Eisenhower, who was born in 1890?
3. What challenges would the "heirs of that first revolution" face in the world of the 1960s?
4. How had the advent of nuclear weapons created a perilous world?
5. Why is the word "vigor" often associated with the Kennedy administration?

Document 7.2. JFK's TV Address During the Cuban Missile Crisis

As our study of the Cold War makes clear, the development of nuclear weapons made the world a very dangerous place. After JFK's failure in 1961 at the Bay of Pigs to topple Cuba's Fidel Castro, the introduction of offensive missals in that communist nation by the Soviet Union produced an explosive clash between Kennedy and Khrushchev. In October 1962, our president addressed the nation about the crisis. His televised speech of October 22 is excerpted next.

> I call upon Chairman Khrushchev to halt and eliminate this clandestine, reckless, and provocative threat to world peace and stable relations between our two countries. I call upon him further to abandon this course of world domination, and to join in an historic effort to end the perilous arms race and to transform the history of man. He has an opportunity to move the world back from the abyss of destruction.

Thinking Historically

1. Did the previous year's Bay of Pigs fiasco create the Cuban Missile Crisis of 1962?
2. How do you think the American people received the revelation that the Soviet Union had placed offensive nuclear weapons in Cuba?
3. What was the message that Kennedy was trying to send Nikita Khrushchev?
4. Was our president attempting to prevent a nuclear showdown with his use of a "quarantine" instead of a military attack on Cuba?
5. Was Kennedy's tone in this televised address intended also to influence those individuals in his administration who favored war?

Document 7.3. Adlai Stevenson's UN Speech

As the Cuban Missile Crisis played out, our ambassador to the UN, Adlai Stevenson, publicly confronted the Soviets with photographic evidence that the nuclear weapons had indeed been placed in Cuba, despite Khrushchev's initial denial. Stevenson alerted the delegates to his belief that this crisis was not just a confrontation between the United States and the Soviet Union but a fundamental "world civil war," a threat to all nations. Here is a portion of his UN comments.

> I regret that people here at the United Nations seem to believe that the cold war is a private struggle between two great superpowers. It isn't a private struggle; it is a world civil war—a contest between the pluralistic world and the monolithic world. ... Every nation that is now independent and wants to remain independent is involved, whether they know it or not.

Thinking Historically

1. Was Ambassador Stevenson's assessment of the Cuban situation accurate?
2. Who in addition to the Soviets was he trying to influence with his comments?
3. Why is the Cold War often viewed as a bi-polar confrontation between "us" and "them"?
4. How would the Soviet Union's UN friends view the situation in Cuba?
5. How close did the events of October 1962 come to igniting World War III?

Document 7.4. Lyndon B. Johnson's War on Poverty

Having served as majority leader of the US Senate before becoming JFK's vice president, LBJ would become remarkably successful as a civil rights president, producing significant legislation that transformed America. He knew how laws were made, and he used his political skills to secure passage of legislation such as the 1964 Civil Rights Act and the Economic Opportunity Act. As we will see in the next chapter, his domestic success was affected by his pursuit of the Vietnam War. In early 1964, however, he boldly declared a war on poverty. His remarks are found next.

> I have called for a national war on poverty. Our objective: total victory.
> There are millions of Americans—one fifth of our people—who have not shared in the abundance which has been granted to most of us, and on whom the gates of opportunity have been closed. ...
> The war on poverty is not a struggle simply to support people, to make them dependent on the generosity of others.
> It is a struggle to give people a chance.

Thinking Historically

1. One of Johnson's mentors was FDR. How is LBJ's war on poverty an extension of Roosevelt's New Deal?
2. What, in your judgment, was our obligation in 1964 to the one-fifth of the population that Johnson mentions as living in poverty?
3. What factors created the need for a broad-based war on poverty?
4. How did Johnson's political skills enable Johnson to achieve legislative success?
5. Why was LBJ's domestic program undermined by his expansion of the war in Southeast Asia?

Document 7.5. Fannie Lou Hamer's Democratic Convention Speech, 1964

As America continued to wrestle with fundamental questions about race and equality, the Democratic Party, LBJ's party, tried to determine a fair representation for African Americans, who were often excluded from power in the Deep South and denied the right to vote. At the 1964 national party convention, Mississippi's Fannie Lou Hamer urged the party to accept more African American delegates. She noted that she was from the same county as the party's two White US senators but that they were blocking federal voting rights legislation and a more representative delegation. She gave an impassioned defense of the need for change in the comments that follow.

> I was in jail when Medgar Evers was murdered. ...
> All of this is on account we want to register, to become first-class citizens, and if the Freedom Democratic Party is not seated now, I question America, in this America, the land of the free and the home of the brave where we have to sleep with our telephones off the hooks because our lives be threatened daily because we want to live as decent human beings, in America?

Thinking Historically

1. While strides were being made in civil rights during the Johnson presidency, why were people like Fannie Lou Hamer frustrated?
2. Why did she find distasteful the word "compromise," which was offered by the Democratic Party?
3. What do Hamer's words tell us about power in the mid-1960s?
4. Were their limits to what LBJ could do for people like Hamer without antagonizing powerful White senators from the South?
5. Is Hamer correct in seeing voting rights as the key to racial fairness in America?

8

ROLLER COASTER

America's involvement in Vietnam went back to the last year of World War II when a clandestine group known as the Deer Team was parachuted in to work in tandem with Ho Chi Minh and other communists who were rescuing American pilots held by the Japanese. The Deer Team and Ho cooperated in this effort, and Ho sought US assistance as the war ended in preventing the return of France, which had controlled the region before Japan seized control. In 1944, FDR seemed sympathetic to independence for Southeast Asia and remarked that France has "milked" its Asian colonies for a century. The onset of the Cold War, however, changed this goal because France was needed as an American ally against the Soviet Union.

Ho and his communist military units fought France, which received American aid, for nearly a decade. In 1954, the communists defeated the French at Dien Bien Phu. Vietnam was divided between communists and noncommunists. An election to reunite the area was scheduled (and never conducted) and into the void tumbled the United States. Slowly, the American military increased its presence in the area. Eisenhower resisted the introduction of our armed forces, but JFK gradually increased the number of "advisers," while searching for a South Vietnamese leader who could defeat Ho. LBJ would ride this roller coaster, which only went higher.

As he announced his war on poverty, Johnson embarked on an escalated war against Vietnamese communists. In August 1964, a series of incidents occurred in the Gulf of Tonkin when communist patrol boats allegedly attacked two vessels, the *USS Mattox* and the *USS Turner Joy*. LBJ went before Congress and received permission "to take all necessary means" to protect Americans. This Gulf of Tonkin Resolution served as the president's justification for increasing America's presence in Vietnam (see Documents 8.1 and 8.2). By March 1965, US Marines landed in Da Nang and 125,000 troops and $1,700,000,000 were authorized to fund action in the area. Communists used well-disciplined North Vietnamese personnel to attack Americans that year at Ia Drang, and the draft supplied still more American soldiers as South Vietnam became a divisive issue for our country.

Other issues were creating tensions. In 1963, Betty Freidan had published her book *The Feminine Mystique*, a criticism of a male-dominated culture, "the problem with no name," she called it. Gender divided the sexes, and others like Gloria Steinem and Helen Gurley Brown with her *Sex and the Single Girl* organized women in the 1960s as they sought respect and equality. The National Organization of Women would be created in 1966. Brown's philosophy of sexual expression eventually found its way onto the pages of her magazine, *Cosmopolitan*.

Throughout 1965, Johnson maneuvered through Congress the Voting Rights Act, a measure that would encounter hostility among White southerners and alter the political dynamics of the Deep South. That year there had been riots in Los Angeles after a police shooting of an African American, resulting in 34 deaths and $40,000,000 in property damages. African Americans were attacked by police in Selma, Alabama, in March of that year on the Edmund Pettus Bridge, a clash known as "Bloody Sunday." Television documented the changes occurring in America and the resistance to it: Women lacking bras and wearing miniskirts. Battered protesters in Alabama.

But it was the Vietnam War that drove a wedge between generations as the draft increased and anti-war protests picked up steam. Johnson attempted to explain the importance of defeating Asian communism while younger Americans became estranged from their government. Dr. King, who had remained supportive as Johnson fought his war against poverty, criticized the Vietnam War in 1967, and Johnson lost the civil rights figure as an ally. King said, "It was time to break silence." King had received the Nobel Peace Prize in 1964 as Johnson was defeating Barry Goldwater for the presidency by more than 15,000,000 votes. CBS television's Walter Cronkite, "the most trusted man in America," raised serious questions about the costly war the following year as casualties skyrocketed.

The war seemed pointless and wasteful to many Americans, despite Johnson's continuous efforts to explain its rationale (see Document 8.3). In January 1968, communists launched the Tet Offensive in South Vietnam. While a failure militarily, the offensive was television news in this nation, and a beleaguered Johnson announced in March that he would not seek reelection. He began peace negotiations in Paris with the communists, but these discussions were slow and full of acrimony. More than 100 college campuses experienced demonstrations. Some buildings were torched. The Students for a Democratic Society were formed to unify those who opposed the conflict. Anti-war candidates like Senator Eugene McCarthy and Senator Robert Kennedy, the slain president's brother, offered themselves as alternatives to the voters, seeking to emphasize the failure of the Johnson administration. Troop totals reached 540,000 as the Democrats ripped themselves apart over the war in Southeast Asia. An American spy vessel, the *USS Pueblo*, was seized off the coast of North Korea earlier that year, illustrating America's weakness.

In April 1968, King was assassinated in Memphis, Tennessee, while leading a labor protest, and riots occurred nationwide. His criticism of what had become "Lyndon's War" had resulted in increased Federal Bureau of Investigation surveillance as the government sought fruitlessly to identify the civil rights figure as a communist. Black Muslim Malcolm X had been fatally shot in 1965, and the nation seemed to be committing suicide. The Great Society, despite its successes, had become a receding mirage.

Robert Kennedy became the rallying point for the young and minority groups, but he, too, fell victim to an assassin's bullet in June 1968 shortly after winning the California Democratic Party primary. The Democrats turned to Johnson's vice president, Hubert Humphrey, and protests erupted in Chicago during the August national convention. Police were seen on television beating protesters outside the convention hall. Weary, the country turned to the Republicans' Richard Nixon, Eisenhower's vice president. Nixon brought with him a questionable reputation because of his political methods, but he called himself "the New Nixon." And he professed to support a "secret plan" for ending the carnage in Vietnam. Narrowly, Nixon triumphed over Humphrey and third-party candidate segregationist George Wallace. LBJ, in a sense, became a casualty of "Lyndon's War" with student protests and political exile. It was hoped as 1969 began that the nation's turbulent roller coaster ride would cease as "the New Nixon" pledged "to bring us together."

Document 8.1. The Gulf of Tonkin Incident

Chapter 8 reminds us that America's Vietnam experience stretched back to a clandestine team that worked closely with communists in 1945 to rescue downed pilots from the Japanese. After World War II, France, an ally of the United States in the Cold War, resumed control of its colonies in Southeast Asia, angering the communist leader Ho Chi Minh who wanted national independence. From 1945 through 1954, Presidents Truman and Eisenhower supplied the French with financial and military aid as they tried to hold on to their Asian empire. Finally, in 1954, the French were defeated at the Battle of Dien Bien Phu. Slowly, America increased its troop presence in the area as Vietnam was divided between pro-Western and communist governments. This commitment saw troop levels increase throughout the Kennedy and Johnson administrations. In 1964, LBJ received approval from Congress to do "anything" to protect American forces. The following is an excerpt from the *Washington Post* about the Gulf of Tonkin Incident of that August.

> An attack on a United States destroyer by three North Vietnamese torpedo boats off that nation's coast yesterday was beaten off by American sea and air gunfire in what Washington treated as a limited incident.
>
> No American casualties or damage resulted, it was announced. Officials said all three Communist boats were believed hit in the first naval engagement of its kind in the Southeast Asia crisis.

Thinking Historically

1. Reading this August 3, 1964, newspaper account, what questions would you have had about the incident?
2. What, exactly, were our strategic goals in Southeast Asia?

3. Why is Vietnam part of the Cold War by the mid-1960s?
4. If you had been a member of the US Congress, what evidence would you have requested about the 1964 Gulf of Tonkin encounter?
5. Why is "roller coaster" a useful metaphor for America's escalating presence in the region, as well as social tensions?

Document 8.2. Johnson's Comments on the Gulf of Tonkin Resolution

Within days, President Johnson told Americans that the incident had occurred twice: initially with the *USS Mattox* and on August 4 with the *USS Turner Joy*. He used his political skills and the power of the presidency to rally support for the Gulf of Tonkin Resolution, which most members and the public endorsed on August 7, 1964. The following is a portion of the president's comments at Syracuse University.

> The attacks were deliberate.
>
> The attacks were unprovoked.
>
> The attacks have been answered. ...
>
> Aggression—deliberate, willful and systemic aggression—has unmasked its face to the entire world. The world remembers—the world must never forget—that aggression unchallenged is aggression unleashed.
>
> We of the United States have not forgotten.
>
> That is why we have answered this aggression.

Thinking Historically

1. What is LBJ trying to accomplish by making these comments on a university campus?
2. Is this speech intended to influence the American people with its allusions to the aggression of the 1930s and 1940s?
3. Why did few Americans challenge the president's account of the need to firmly respond to the attacks, which, in hindsight, are questionable?
4. Why were most Americans focused on other challenges in 1964, such as the civil rights movement?
5. Why did Johnson almost immediately fall victim to what has been called "a credibility gap" in Vietnam?

Document 8.3. Johnson's Defense of the Vietnam War

Within a year, the US Marines had come ashore at Da Nang and Johnson supported his generals' request for thousands more troops. Again, in 1965, the president used the stage of a university, Johns Hopkins University, to try to explain his rationale for the war. By that year, students were beginning to express opposition to the conflict because they were being drafted into military service as casualties rose. They questioned the war in increasing numbers, and as Chapter 8 makes clear, the roller coaster continued to zoom, dividing the country for the remainder of Johnson's White House tenure. The following is an excerpt from the president's Johns Hopkins's remarks.

> Why are we in Vietnam? We are there because we have a promise to keep. Since 1954 every American president has offered support to the people of South Vietnam. We have helped to build, and we have helped to defend. Thus, over the years, we have made a national pledge to help South Vietnam defend its independence. And I intend to keep our promise.
>
> To dishonor that pledge, to abandon this small and brave nation to its enemy, and to the terror that must follow, would be an unforgivable wrong.

Thinking Historically

1. As a college student in 1965, would you have been convinced that America's escalating presence was a question of "honor"?
2. Why did the public differ on the need to send troops to this faraway place?
3. What, exactly, were our "promises" in this Cold War conflict?
4. A seasoned politician, LBJ seems to be missing a gradual change in opinion. Why?
5. How did Johnson's conduct of our presence in Southeast Asia endanger his war on poverty and his commitment to civil rights?

9

MALAISE

President Richard Nixon's "secret plan" for ending the Vietnam War was "Vietnamization," a gradual exit from the region by our troops while providing our anti-communist allies with air support and weapons. Throughout 1969, this Nixon Doctrine, part of the Cold War, was on display in Southeast Asia, but the voices of the anti-war movement continued domestically while troop numbers slowly declined from a high of more than 500,000. The increasingly unpopular war, with 400 fatalities per week in 1968, had devastated the Johnson presidency, and it consumed his successor, too, as we will see in this chapter.

Our nation's journey into outer space, a promise made by JFK in 1961, climaxed in 1969, fulfilling the slain president's promise in that year. Three American astronauts reached the moon in the summer of 1969. Neil Armstrong stepped on the lunar surface that July, proclaiming it "one small step for a man, one giant leap for mankind." America watched on television as Armstrong planted an American flag and collected samples from the surface. Nixon telephoned the astronauts from the White House, congratulating them for their success in history's longest distance telephone call (see Document 9.1).

That year, gay Americans were raided at a popular New York City club called the Stonewall Inn, sparking neighborhood clashes between police and patrons. Intolerance, as we have witnessed, is a theme in our history. Since 1969, there has been much progress in the area of lesbian, gay, bisexual, transgender, queer, or questioning freedom, but in June 1969 this journey was in its infancy. Gender equality has been slow and not without violence and displays of intolerance, such as that displayed during the Stonewall Inn riot in Greenwich Village.

While Armstrong and his fellow astronauts, Buzz Aldrin and Michael Collins, were celebrating their success, the last of the Kennedy brothers, Senator Edward Kennedy was immersed in a tragic death. His automobile passenger, the slain Robert Kennedy's aide Mary Jo Kopechne, drowned in Massachusetts when Senator Kennedy's car veered off a bridge at Chappaquiddick. She died, and Kennedy's political ambitions for a future bid for the White House died also because of his recklessness and his delay in notifying authorities.

As the fall semester of 1969 approached, 500,000 mostly young Americans gathered in August near Bethel, New York, at Woodstock for a music festival. The music was rock and roll, seasoned with anti-war lyrics. Jimmy Hendrix, Janis Joplin, Joe Cocker, and other legends performed as the crowd camped. Some older Americans were displeased with the displays of the crowd, which often used illegal drugs and practiced "free love" that weekend. Two years earlier, the young had gathered in San Francisco for "the summer of love." Television images of these events disconcerted older Americans.

The war, however, did not stop. Vietnamization was slow. In the spring of 1970, Nixon launched an "incursion" into Cambodia and Laos, which triggered anger on college campuses (Document 9.2). His purpose was to eradicate communist sanctuaries in those two Asian nations, but American students saw it as an expansion of the war. In early May, violence erupted at Kent State University when members of the Ohio National Guard, many of whom were young, fired on protesting students. Five students died in the Kent State Massacre, and our conflict now became "Nixon's War."

The integration of America's public schools continued at a slow pace. In 1971, the US Supreme Court ruled in *Swann v. Charlotte-Mecklenburg* that school buses could be used to integrate the schools by transporting racially diverse students to various schools. Federal funds were terminated for school districts that resisted fulfilling the court's *Brown* mandate of 1954. Racial equality, like gender equality, has been a slow process and not without resistance, as this book notes in previous chapters.

By 1972, Nixon embarked on several missions: to continue Vietnamization, to secure reelection, to negotiate an arms reduction treaty with the Soviets, and to boldly reach out to the communist Chinese. With the assistance of Secretary of State Henry Kissinger, the president met with China's Chairman Mao and Zhou Enlai in Beijing and began the acceptance of China into the world community. A visit that year to the Great Wall was a spectacular demonstration of a changing world. Nixon left his reelection campaign to his Committee to Re-elect the President (CREEP), and this group engaged in illegal activities, most significantly the June 1972 break-in at Democratic Party headquarters, located in Washington's Watergate building. While the burglars were apprehended, the Watergate affair would lead to the demise of the Nixon presidency.

Two reporters for the *Washington Post*, Bob Woodward and Carl Bernstein, wrote in their newspaper about the burglars, trying to ascertain the president's involvement in a series of questionable actions during his reelection campaign, such as soliciting illegal campaign contributions, pursuit of the leakers who had released "The Pentagon Papers" that documented our lengthy involvement in Southeast Asia, and abuse of power. Congress began to probe these matters, even though Nixon glided to reelection over the anti-war Senator George McGovern of South Dakota. Congressional hearings revealed that Nixon tape-recorded his conversations, and Congress battled to gain access to these recordings.

As Document 0.3 explains, the 1973 US Supreme Court *Roe v. Wade* decision extended abortion rights to women across America. This issue remains divisive with pro-choice people opposed by pro-life advocates. In January of that year, at the Paris Peace Conference, Kissinger, our South Vietnamese allies, and the communists signed an agreement, which withdrew most of our remaining troops from the region (Document 9.3). American prisoners of war were released by the communists, and Nixon considered it "peace with honor" despite the fact that in 1975, South Vietnam would fall to the communists.

Nixon's presidency was also collapsing. In the summer of 1974, his tape recordings were turned over to Congress; they documented numerous examples of illegal actions, as well as vulgar Oval Office conversations (Document 9.4). Heading toward certain impeachment, Nixon resigned his office in August, succeeded by his vice president Gerald Ford, who that September pardoned his predecessor amid a public uproar. The economy was in a recession because of the 1973 war in the Middle East and a hike in gasoline prices by the newly created Organization of Petroleum Exporting Countries (OPEC). America's steady support of the modern state of Israel, which stretched back to the Truman years, now became economically costly. Ford seemed unable to pull the nation out of the recession, with its double-digit interest rates and inflation, as America's bicentennial approached in 1976.

Ford had spent his entire career in Washington, as a Michigan member of Congress, as Nixon's vice president briefly, and as president presiding over a recession, as well as the aforementioned collapse of South Vietnam. The voters turned in 1976 to a former Georgia governor, Jimmy Carter, who promised "to never lie to us." Carter was an outsider, not tainted by Vietnam, Watergate, or an anemic economy. As he and his family walked down Pennsylvania Avenue in January 1977, it was hoped that this change in direction would revitalize America.

As an outsider, Carter brought many aides, "the Georgia Mafia," to Washington. Inexperience became a problem, and Carter's support for the 1978 Panama Canal Treaty, which returned control of that facility to Panama in 1999, angered some people, as did the lingering recession. But that year, Carter began negotiations with Israel and Egypt, seeking to achieve peace in that troubled region. The agreement, the Camp David Accords, stands as a crowning achievement of the Carter presidency, careful international diplomacy between two historic enemies. Bringing the leaders of the two nations to Washington in 1978 remains a testament to Carter's skill and persistence.

It is ironic that the Middle East and the continuing Cold War would derail Carter. One of our allies, the shah of Iran, had cooperated with us from his strategic nation, which borders the Soviet Union. We trained his secret police, SAVAK, which brutalized Iranians. When he became ill in 1978, we permitted him to seek medical treatment in America, despite the warnings of religious leaders who came to power in 1979. The Islamic Revolution toppled the shah and triggered the seizure of the American embassy in Tehran. Fifty-two Americans were held hostage for 444 days. A failed rescue attempt in 1980 made Carter appear impotent to the world and to the theocrats who now controlled Iran. Images broadcast nightly on television from Tehran and a futile attempt by Edward Kennedy to challenge Carter for the Democratic Party's 1980 nomination illustrated Carter's weakness, as did the continuing high oil prices, which exceeded $1.00 per gallon.

While Carter never used the actual word "malaise," it seems a fitting description of the national mood in post-Vietnam, post-Watergate America with all of its social tensions. Thus, it was understandable that California's ex-governor Ronald Reagan, a vigorous former Hollywood actor, would garner support when he vowed that "America would never be held hostage" under a Reagan presidency. Until he left office in January 1981, Carter tried unsuccessfully to gain freedom for the Iranian hostages. It was not until Reagan was inaugurated on January 20, however, that they were released. A final rebuke from the theocracy of Iran and punishment for our loyalty to the shah.

Document 9.1. Neil Armstrong Walks on the Moon

JFK's bold pledge in 1961 to reach the moon consumed much of the decade. Astronauts from the United States and cosmonauts from the Soviet Union competed to dominate outer space. Three Americans died tragically in preparation for the goal. By 1969, however, our nation succeeded in reaching the lunar surface. As this chapter notes, Neil Armstrong set foot on the moon that July. The following is the iconic announcement by Armstrong to Mission Control.

> That's one small step for a man, one giant leap for mankind. The surface is fine and powdery. I can pick it up loosely with my toe. It does adhere in fine layers like powdered charcoal to the sole and inside of my boots. I only go in a small fraction of an inch—an eighth of an inch—but I can see the footprints of my boots and the treads in the fine sandy particles.

Thinking Historically

1. In a tumultuous decade, why was this dramatic event a source of national pride?
2. Was the race to the moon worth the cost in resources and lives?
3. How does our success fit into the context of the Cold War with the Soviet Union?
4. Why are Neil Armstrong's initial comments iconic?
5. Why have we not returned to the moon in nearly 50 years?

Document 9.2. Richard Nixon's Incursion Announcement

As we have reviewed, America's longest war consumed several presidencies, most notably the Johnson and Nixon administrations. The latter adhered to the policy of Vietnamization, but the gradual reduction of troop commitments was divisive, especially among the young. In 1970, President Richard Nixon announced an "incursion" into Cambodia and Laos. College campuses erupted in demonstrations that spring. The following is the president's explanation.

> (Cambodia) has sent a call to the United States, to a number of other nations, for assistance. Because if the enemy effort succeeds, Cambodia would become a vast enemy staging area and a springboard for attacks on South Vietnam along 600 miles of frontier—a refuge where enemy troops could return from combat without fear of retaliation.
>
> North Vietnamese men and supplies could then be poured into that country, jeopardizing not only the lives of our own men but the people of South Vietnam as well.

Thinking Historically

1. Explain President Nixon's rationale for the April 1970 "incursion" into Cambodia and Laos.
2. Was his decision an "incursion" or an "invasion"?
3. As an 18-year-old college student in 1970, what would have been your reaction to the president's decision?
4. Why did Vietnamization take so long and why was it divisive?
5. Why did Congress in 1973 restrict the president's power to unilaterally launch such incursions?

Document 9.3. Nixon Announces "Peace With Honor" in Vietnam

The slow pace of Vietnamization reached a decisive moment in January 1973 when Richard Nixon announced to the nation that the Paris Peace Accords would bring the remaining 27,000 American troops home, as well as the prisoners of war held by the communists. By this point, over 58,000 Americans had died in Southeast Asia, and the war had become our nation's longest and costliest. Nixon had secured reelection the previous November and had visited both communist China and the Soviet Union in 1972. The conduct of his reelection effort, however, would lead to Nixon's resignation the following summer. South Vietnam would fall to the communists in the spring of 1975 under the presidency of Gerald Ford. In the following, Nixon announces the Paris Peace Accords.

> Good evening. I have asked for this radio and television time tonight for the purpose of announcing that we today have concluded an agreement to end the war and bring peace with honor in Vietnam and in Southeast Asia. …
>
> We must recognize that ending the war is only the first step toward building the peace. All parties must now see to it that this is a peace that lasts, and also a peace that heals, and a peace that not only ends the

war in Southeast Asia, but contributes to the prospects of peace in the whole world.

Thinking Historically

1. How would you describe the tone of the president's remarks? Naïve? Realistic? Deceptive?
2. Why did South Vietnam's government have to be pressured by Washington to sign the Paris Peace Accords?
3. What was achieved by our country's involvement in Southeast Asia?
4. In your judgment, was Nixon hoping that his foreign policy initiatives, including this agreement, would overshadow the Watergate crimes?
5. What lessons should we learn from America's Vietnam experience?

Document 9.4. Nixon's White House Tapes

Throughout Nixon's presidency, his aides harassed political enemies, bugged opponents, squeezed campaign contributions from companies that did business with the federal government, intimidated the press, compiled an "enemies list," and condoned the 1972 break-in at Democratic Party headquarters in the Watergate Complex in Washington. The burglars were paid hush money to not cooperate with the authorities. The 1974 release of tape-recorded conversations revealed that the president was intimately involved in a cover-up of what, collectively, was called "Watergate." In the following excerpt, he speaks on March 13, 1973, with his White House counsel, John Dean, who eventually testified against him before Congress.

> Nixon: "How much of a crisis? It will be—I am thinking in terms of—the point is everything is a crisis. (expletive deleted) it is a terrible lousy thing—it will remain a crisis among the upper intellectual types, the soft heads, our own, too—Republicans—and the Democrats and the rest. Average people won't think it is much of a crisis unless it affects them."

Thinking Historically

1. This conversation occurred just two months after the announcement of the Paris Peace Accords. Why does Nixon believe "average people" will not care about his political conduct?
2. The tape recordings reveal a vulgar, inarticulate, mean, petty, calculating president. Why did the 1974 release of the tapes doom the Nixon presidency?
3. Did the Watergate crimes stain the office of the president for future occupants?
4. Is there a correlation between the tumult of the era and the Nixon presidency?
5. Was Gerald Ford correct to pardon Nixon for his political actions?

Document 9.5. Jimmy Carter's Call for Energy Conservation

This chapter makes clear that Jimmy Carter, a Washington outsider, inherited the debris of an unpopular war, failed presidencies, and an anemic economy. The latter was reflected in high energy costs and high interest rates. In July 1979, Carter spoke to the nation about his goals and the importance of uniting as America wrestled with its challenges. He urged energy conservation and the development of alternative energy sources. Excerpted below are his televised comments. Unfortunately, things would get worse that year with the seizure of the American embassy in Iran.

> Energy will be the immediate test of our ability to unite this nation, and it can also be the standard around which we rally. On the battlefield of energy we can win for our nation a new confidence, and we can seize control again of our common destiny.

Thinking Historically

1. Was Carter correct that we must step away from our dependence on oil from the Middle East as a major source of energy?
2. Why is this speech often called the president's "malaise" speech even though he never uses that word?
3. Did Carter's lack of Washington experience hinder his effectiveness with Congress?
4. Why did his success the previous year in making peace between Israel and Egypt with the Camp David Accords not increase his popularity with the American people?
5. Comment on whether Carter had little control over the events that created the dismal national mood as the 1980 presidential election approached.

10

MORNING

While Ronald Reagan's election in 1980 signaled a new direction for America, the tensions of the Cold War remained. When the Soviet Union attempted to bolster an ally in Afghanistan in 1979 by invading that country, Jimmy Carter responded by boycotting the 1980 Olympics in Moscow. Reagan would be more assertive. He armed the Muslims who were fighting the Soviets in Afghanistan with weapons and shared intelligence. The Reagan administration was determined to aggressively resist communists there and elsewhere. He outlined his view of the world, as well as his economic philosophy, which tilted toward the wealthy, in his January 20, 1981, inaugural address (Document 10.1).

With his ability as a communicator, Reagan partnered with the United Kingdom's prime minister Margaret Thatcher, a conservative, to form a Western alliance against Soviet expansion (see Document 10.2). He and Thatcher remained steadfast in their criticism of what Reagan called "the evil empire." His presidency, however, was almost terminated unexpectedly in March 1981 when an assassin seriously wounded him and others outside a Washington hotel where Reagan had made a speech. He recovered, nonetheless, waving from the hospital window with First Lady Nancy Reagan by his side. Even with a bullet wound dangerously close to his heart, the 68-year-old former movie actor projected a robust, fearless image.

Later in 1981, Reagan fired 11,345 striking air traffic controllers, demonstrating his view of a president's powers. However, there were limits to Reagan's powers, as the tragic suicide bombing of a barracks in Beirut, Lebanon, which cost the lives of 241 Marines, demonstrated. The Middle East was a dangerous place, even to a commander in chief who had survived a near assassination. That suicide attack was followed by an invasion of the Caribbean nation of Grenada, where a communist government had come to power. This conflict, Reagan explained, was a threat to US citizens attending medical school in Grenada. That year, Reagan announced his support for the Strategic Defensive Initiative (SDI), otherwise known as "Star Wars," which Reagan believed would shield the United States from a Soviet nuclear attack. It would be a costly venture, and the Soviets responded by boycotting the 1984 Olympic games in Los Angeles, California.

Running for reelection in 1984, Reagan talked of it being "Morning in America." The economy had weathered a recession in 1981 through 1983; we were committed to challenging, or perhaps financially wrecking, the Soviet Union (Document 10.3). But there would be a major stumble in 1986 when word leaked of a Reagan plan to assist anti-communist forces in Nicaragua by selling weapons to Iran, which was fighting a war with Iraq, with the profits going to the anti-communists, the Contras, in Nicaragua. The Iran-Contra Affair bypassed the Boland Amendment whereby Congress had prohibited such American aid (Document 10.4). As Congress investigated, it became clear that Reagan had permitted the arrangement to receive American aid. Reagan told the American people that he had not "intended" to supply weapons to the Nicaraguan Contras.

By the end of his presidency, Reagan had met with the Soviet Union's Mikhail Gorbachev to try to reduce the arsenal of weapons both countries possessed. Gorbachev was presiding over a country in dire economic condition because of a flawed system of government and the pressures of Star Wars. Personally, the two leaders seemed to get along, but it was obvious to the world that communism in the Soviet Union was collapsing. It would be Reagan's successor, George H. W. Bush, who would be in office in 1989 when the Berlin Wall was breached and Eastern Europe, behind the iron curtain that Winston Churchill had articulated in 1946, was removed as the Soviet Union retreated from the Cold War (see Document 10.5).

Bush appointed Clarence Thomas to the US Supreme Court in 1991, amid charges leveled at the nominee of sexual harassment by Thomas's former aide, Anita Hill. The confirmation hearings presided over by Delaware Senator Joe Biden, raised the specter of race, with Thomas telling the television audience he was the subject of "a high-tech lynching." Narrowly, Thomas was confirmed.

In 1990, Iraq invaded oil-rich Kuwait. Bush mobilized a United Nations coalition the following year to liberate Kuwait and to protect our ally Saudi Arabia in an operation called Desert Storm. America had become the last remaining superpower. Communist China, which had taken a seat on the UN Security Council in 1975, ousting Taiwan, brutally thwarted a demonstration in Beijing in 1989. The world remained a very dangerous place, even with the Soviet empire transformed into "Russia" and a few allied nations.

A recession in 1992 prevented Bush from securing reelection, and the country turned to Arkansas governor Bill Clinton. Instability manifested the following year when American military personnel were attacked in the African nation of Sudan. *Black Hawk Down* was written about the attack. More unrest occurred in Rwanda and the former communist nation of Yugoslavia, which had been split into feuding ethnic groups during the Clinton years.

Clinton battled a resurgent Republican Party in 1994, which was led by Speaker of the House Newt Gingrich. His "Contract with America" emphasized lower taxes and reduced size of the federal government. A government shutdown over the budget in 1995 inadvertently created a situation that almost derailed the Clinton presidency. A 22-two-year-old White House intern Monica Lewinsky commenced an affair with Clinton during the shutdown. Clinton's promiscuous life and his perjury in a similar sexual matter led to his 1997 impeachment, which failed when it reached the US Senate's trial phase.

For the remainder of his presidency, Clinton and First Lady Hillary Clinton tried to project an image of domestic peace as the economy surged, but the sordid details of the Lewinsky affair hovered over the country and the couple. It damaged his vice president's chances to succeed him. In 2000, Vice President Al Gore narrowly lost to Texas governor George W. Bush, the son of the former president. The election was disputed with Gore ahead in popular votes, but the Supreme Court awarded Florida's electoral votes to Bush. The twenty-first century commenced with the United States hoping to lay to rest the spectacle of the embarrassing impeachment of Bill Clinton. The year 2001 would be remembered, however, for a surprise attack in New York, Washington, and in the skies over Pennsylvania, not by "the evil empire" of Ronald Reagan's time but by Islamic terrorists, hijacking jets and aiming them at landmarks such as New York's World Trade Center and Washington's Pentagon, resulting in the tragic loss of nearly 3,000 American lives on the morning of September 11, 2001, as well as creating a dangerous new era in America's history (see Document 10.6).

Document 10.1. Ronald Reagan's Economic Philosophy

The Carter administration had been plagued by an anemic economy that it inherited from Gerald Ford. Double-digit interest rates, skyrocketing oil prices, and high inflation sapped the nation's vitality. Making matters worse was the 444-day Iranian hostage situation. All of these factors defeated Jimmy Carter and led to Reagan's inauguration on January 20, 1981. Boldly, he conveyed to the citizens the need to alter the downward spiral of the United States and use a different economic model, one with low taxes and increased defense spending, to energize the nation. In the following, we can sense Reagan's philosophy.

> In this present crisis, government is not the solution to our problem. Government is the problem. ...
>
> It is my intention to curb the size and influence of the federal establishment and to demand recognition of the distinction between the powers granted to the federal government and those reserved to the states or to the people.
>
> All of us need to be reminded that the federal government did not create the states; the states created the federal government.

Thinking Historically

1. Explain Ronald Reagan's view of the state versus the federal government.
2. How does the new president's philosophy of government differ from that of Franklin Roosevelt and Lyndon Johnson?

3. Who would benefit from a revised tax structure with relief for big businesses?
4. What citizens would question Reagan's advocacy of trickle-down economics?
5. Why did his new vice president, George H. W. Bush, call the Reagan plan "voodoo economics" when he challenged Reagan for the 1980 Republican Party nomination?

Document 10.2. Reagan's Optimism on Democracy

One of Reagan's foreign policy allies was Great Britain's prime minister Margaret Thatcher, a fellow cold warrior. In a 1982 speech before the House of Commons, the new president summoned forth the memory of Winston Churchill who, as this book reminds us, warned the Western nations about the "iron curtain" of communism that descended on the Soviet Union's East European satellite nations. These comments convey Reagan's optimism about the eventual triumph of democracy.

> We're approaching the end of a bloody century plagued by a terrible political invention—totalitarianism. Optimism comes less easily today, not because democracy is less vigorous, but because democracy's enemies have refined their instruments of repression. Yet optimism is in order because day by day democracy is proving itself to be a not at all fragile flower.

Thinking Historically

1. Is Reagan's interpretation of the Cold War accurate?
2. Why does the American president hope to rally Great Britain to his cause?
3. How can Reagan express optimism at this point in the Cold War?
4. Does Reagan see the 1980s as the definitive decade in the conflict between the United States and our friends and the Soviet Union?
5. Knowing what we know today, why did the "evil empire" collapse by 1989?

Document 10.3. Brzezinski's Support for DSI

Reagan's strengthening of the military and rattling the saber of the SDI gained an ally in the support of Carter's former National Security Adviser, Zbigniew Brzezinski. A hardliner, Brzezinski stood with the president in his advocacy of wrecking the Soviet Union's economy by forcing that nation to spend funds to develop its own costly weapons system. A former professor, Brzezinski saw the SDI initiative as part of the historic rivalry between two very different systems of government: one based on democracy and one grounded in totalitarianism. Next, we see that he sought in 1985 to answer Reagan's foreign policy critics.

Indeed, the time has come for the United States to bite the bullet on the SDI question. Only if a strategic defense system is deployable within the next decade or so, and only if our will to deploy it is proven credible, can the United States trade it for a genuine and comprehensive arms control agreement with the Soviets. It is essential that this system be capable of disrupting and rendering militarily useless a Soviet first strike by intercepting missiles early in flight or knocking them out as they descend toward the United States.

Thinking Historically

1. What, exactly, worried the Soviet Union about Reagan's expensive SDI system?
2. Why did Brzezinski's support strengthen Reagan's plans?
3. Why did proponents of peace with the Soviets criticize the SDI?
4. Was the militarizing of outer space a dangerous proposition?
5. Why did the SDI prove to be eventually unnecessary?

Document 10.4. The Boland Amendment

The Congress's reaction to the undeclared war in Southeast Asia was demonstrated in the 1973 War Powers Act, which required the commander in chief to adhere to a restrictive timetable for the commitment of our military in foreign combat. While Richard Nixon objected, Congress was determined to prevent the use of our troops without a clear statement of purpose and to guarantee congressional oversight of the use of America's military. This position was reiterated in the Reagan presidency with the 1982 and 1984 Boland Amendment, which focused specifically on Central America and the Contras' activities in Nicaragua against the communist government. As this chapter explains, the Reagan administration found a way through Iran-Contra to bypass the Boland statute.

> No appropriations or funds made available pursuant to this joint resolution to the Central Intelligence Agency, the Department of Defense, or any other agency or entity of the United States involved in intelligence activities may be obligated or expended for the purpose or which could have the effect of supporting, directly or indirectly, military or paramilitary operations in Nicaragua by any nation, group, organization, movement or individual.

Thinking Historically

1. Why did the excesses of presidents such as Lyndon Johnson and Richard Nixon during the Vietnam War persuade Congress to adopt the Boland Amendment?
2. What should be the appropriate limits to a president's constitutional powers as commander in chief?
3. Why did the Reagan administration seek ways to circumvent this legislation?
4. Was the Iran-Contra funding arrangement a violation of the Boland Amendment?
5. How did Ronald Reagan escape impeachment for permitting this arrangement to occur?

Document 10.5. The End of the Cold War

For nearly half a century, the Cold War raged between the United States and the Soviet Union. There were numerous "hot spots" in this conflict: the Korean Police Action of 1950 through 1953, the 1962 Cuban Missile Crisis, Southeast Asia, the Middle East, and the Iran-Contra Affair. Two very different economic systems, one capitalist and one a totalitarian command economy competed. As we have seen, both America and the Soviets possessed nuclear weapons. But by the presidency of George H. W. Bush, the flaws in the Soviet Union toppled the communists and, whether or not because of Ronald Reagan's costly SDI, the Berlin Wall was breached in 1989, and the weakness of the Soviets was on display. Even before that final act in the Cold War occurred, the *New York Times* published its analysis of this new era.

> The cold war of poisonous Soviet-American feelings, of domestic political hysteria, of events enlarged and distorted by East-West confrontation, of almost perpetual diplomatic deadlock is over.
>
> The we-they world that emerged after 1945 is giving way to the more traditional struggles of great powers. That contest is more manageable. It permits serious negotiations. It creates new possibilities—for cooperation in combating terrorism, the spread of chemical weapons and common threats to the environment, and for shaping a less violent world.

Thinking Historically

1. Was the *New York Times*'s elation a bit premature?
2. What is your analysis of the Cold War as the twentieth century ended?
3. How, exactly, did the Western nations triumph?
4. What was the fatal flaw in the communist system?
5. Looking at the world of the present, is the Cold War over or merely transformed?

Document 10.6. George W. Bush's 9/11 Address

The surprise attacks of September 11, 2001, shook America's foundation. Nineteen terrorists hijacked four planes that Tuesday morning and aimed them at landmarks: the New York World Trade Building's two towers, the Pentagon in Washington, and at the capitol itself, which was spared by courageous passengers who fought back as that plane made its way toward the People's House where Congress meets. There were 2,977 fatalities, more than at Pearl Harbor seven decades earlier. Six thousand more people were injured, and thousands more have died from various illnesses since September 11. An estimated $10,000,000,000 in property damages were incurred. The terrorists were allied with Al-Qaeda, an Islamic group based in Afghanistan and led by Osama bin Laden, who would be tracked down in 2011 in Pakistan by a special operations unit and killed. On the evening of September 11,

President George W. Bush spoke to the American people. The following is an excerpt from his address.

> This is a day when all Americans from every walk of life unite in our resolve for justice and peace. America has stood down enemies before, and we will do so this time. None of us will ever forget this day. Yet, we go forward to defend freedom and all that is good and just in our world.
> Thank you. Good night. And God bless America.

Thinking Historically

1. Since the World Trade tower had been the site of a 1993 terrorist incident, should we have been more vigilant on 9/11?
2. Did President Bush set the right tone in his remarks to the nation?
3. Was he preparing the nation for a long and costly war on terrorism?
4. What were the root causes of the tragic events of 9/11?
5. Why does America still vividly remember that day?

Conclusion: Walls and Towers

This anthology began with our consideration of the bold entrepreneurs, those captains of industry who with the sweat of the brows of industrial workers, laid the foundation for modern America. These people created a nation, which, by 1898, found itself a world power with an overseas empire. It is a wonderful story of dreams, conflict, justice and injustice, inclusion and exclusion. It is a story of ordinary people like Mississippi's Fannie Lou Hamer, who stood her ground and had her say at the 1964 Democratic Party Convention. Also, it is the story of two world wars with the scholarly Woodrow Wilson and the innovative FDR. And it is the saga of a faraway Cold War effort in Southeast Asia.

Much happened to us and the world from 1877 through 2001. Walls like the one in Berlin were breached, and the iron curtain of communism was raided. Presidents came and left, some of whom had stumbles along the way. Vietnam for Lyndon Johnson and Watergate for Richard Nixon. Iran-Contra for Ronald Reagan. Advances occurred in civil rights, gender equality, and basic human dignity.

As the previous chapter reminds us, on September 11, 2001, we suffered a national blow to our psyche. The hazards of the Middle East continue to be real, even as we mourn those who died in New York City when the World Trade Center's towers were engulfed in flames. A generation earlier, Jimmy Carter was engulfed by the hostage crisis despite the fact that he had brought peace between Israel and Egypt with the 1978 Camp David Accords, a diplomatic triumph that remains in the Middle East.

FDR once explained America's history as plotting events on a sheet of graft paper. There are low points, he said, but there are far more positive moments. By considering the themes of America, we see the negatives and the positives. Walls have, unfortunately, separated us, but they are not permanent. The readers of this book, as we proceed through the twenty-first century, have the potential to continue demolishing the walls that divide us in the world in which we live.

Document C.1. Map of the World, 2000

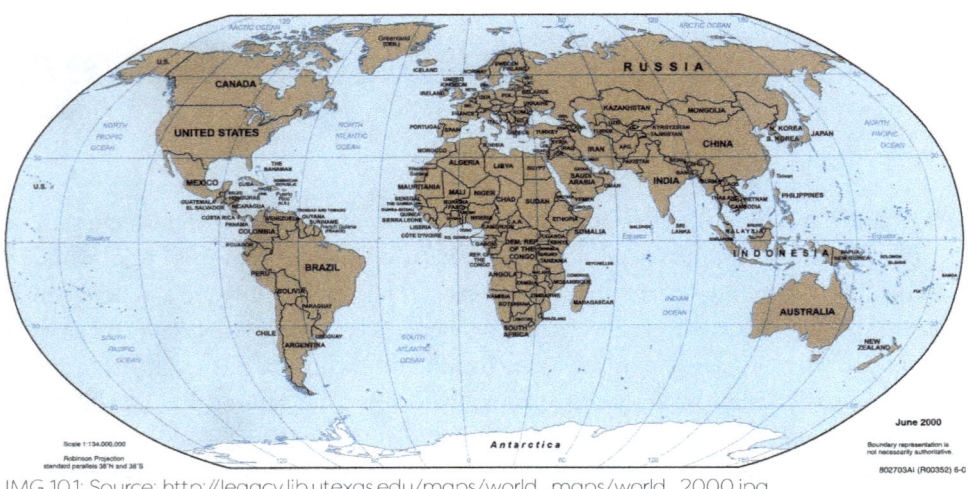

IMG 10.1: Source: http://legacy.lib.utexas.edu/maps/world_maps/world_2000.jpg.

Thinking Historically

1. Compare this map to the one found in this anthology, Document 1.4. How are they similar? How do they differ?
2. How has the changing world created challenges and opportunities for America?
3. What errors have we made?
4. What successes have we made?
5. What should be America's world mission in the twenty-first century?

Document Sources

Boorstin, Daniel J. 1985. *An American Primer.* Chicago: University of Chicago.

Brown v. the Board of Education of Topeka, 347 U.S. 483 (1954).

Brzezinski, Zbigniew. "A Star Wars Solution," *New Republic*, 193, no. 2, July 8, 1985, pp. 16–18.

Bush, George W. "Bush's Remarks to the Nation on Terrorist Attacks," *The New York Times*, September 12, 2001, p. 4.

Carnegie, Andrew. 1886. *Triumphant Democracy.* New York: Scribner's.

Carter, Jimmy. 1980. *Public Papers of the Presidents of the United States: Jimmy Carter, 1979.* Washington, DC: Office of the Federal Register.

Churchill, Winston. "Mr. Churchill's Message," *The New York Times*, March 6, 1946, p. 26.

Congressional Record, 56th Congress, 1st session, vol. 33, 704 (1900).

Congressional Record, 81st Congress, vol. 96, part 2 (1950).

DuBois, W.E.B. 1903. "Of Mr. Booker T. Washington and Others." In *Souls of Black Folk*, pp. 50–5. Chicago: A.C. McClung.

Eisenhower, Dwight. 1961. *Public Papers of the Presidents: Dwight D. Eisenhower 1960–1961*, no. 421. Washington, DC: Office of the Federal Register.

Eisenhower, Dwight D. Address of September 24, 1957, in *Vital Speeches*, vol. 24, 12 (October 15, 1957).

Evans, Hiram W. 1926. "The Klan's Fight for Americanism." *North American Review* 223 (March), p. 26.

Farrer, Fred. "Armstrong Takes 1st Step on Moon," *Chicago Tribune*, July 21, 1969.

Fitzgerald, F. Scott. 1925. *The Great Gatsby.* New York: Scribner's.

Ford, Henry. 1929. *My Philosophy of Industry (An Authorized Interview by Fay Leone Faurote).* New York: Coward McCann.

Harding, Warren B. "Text of President Harding's Inaugural Address," *The New York Times*, March 5, 1921, p. 4.

Hearings Before the Committee of the Judiciary, House of Representatives, 93rd Congress, 2nd sess. (1974).

Johnson, Lyndon B. "Text of Address Given by Johnson at Hopkins," *Washington Post*, April 8, 1965, p. 16.

Johnson, Lyndon B. 1964. *Public Papers of the Presidents of the United States: Lyndon B. Johnson, 1963–1964*, vol. 1. Washington, DC: Office of the Federal Register.

Johnson, Lyndon B. "Johnson's Talk on Syracuse Campus," *The New York Times*, August 6, 1964, p. 7.

Kennedy, John F. 1962. *Public Papers of the Presidents of the United States: John F. Kennedy, 1961*, no. 1. Washington, DC: Office of the Federal Register.

Kennedy, John F. 1963. *Public Papers of the Presidents of the United States: John F. Kennedy, January 1 to December 31, 1962*. Washington, DC: Office of the Federal Register.

"Leadership at the Five and Ten," *Greensboro Daily News*, February 5, 1960.

LeSueur, Meridel. 1932. "Women on the Breadlines." *New Masses* 7 (January).

Marder, Murrey. "Reds' Torpedo Vessels Believed Hit in Fleeing; No American Casualties," *Washington Post*, August 3, 1964, p. 1.

Mills, Kay. 1993. *This Little Light of Mine*. New York: Signet.

Powderly, Terence V. 1890. *Thirty Years of Labor*. Columbus, OH: Excelsior Publishing House.

Public Law No. 98-441, 98 Statute 1699 (1984).

Reagan, Ronald. 1983. *Public Papers of the Presidents of the United States: Ronald Reagan, 1982*. Washington, DC: Office of the Federal Register.

Riis, Jacob. 1890. *How the Other Half Lives*. New York: Scribner's.

Roe v. Wade, 410 U.S. 113 (1973).

Roosevelt, Franklin D. "Text of the Inaugural Address; President for Vigorous Action," *The New York Times*, March 5, 1933, p. 1.

Roosevelt, Franklin D. "Text of Roosevelt's Alien Order," *The New York Times*, February 20, 1942, p. 6.

Roosevelt, Theodore. "Roosevelt Idea of a Good Citizen," *The New York Times*, April 24, 1910, p. 9.

"Soviet Political Agreements and Results. The Words of American Statesman who Negotiated with Soviet Representatives since 1959," *Staff Study for the Subcommittee to Investigate the Administration of the Internal Security Act and Other Internal Security Laws of the Committee on the Judiciary*, United States Senate, Volume II. Washington: U.S. Government Printing Office, 1964.

"The Cold War is Over," *The New York Times*, April 2, 1989, p. 30.

Truman, Harry S. "President Truman's Radio Address on Korea, U.S. Far Eastern Policy," *The New York Times*, April 12, 1951, p. 4.

"United States Statutes at Large," vol. 71, U.S. Government Printing Office, 1957, p. 5-6.

U.S. Department of State, *Addresses and Messages of Franklin D. Roosevelt*, Senate Document No. 188, 77th Cong., 2nd sess., 21-4.

Weekly Compilation of Presidential Documents 6 (1970), 597.

Weekly Compilation of Presidential Documents 9 (1973), 43.

Weisman, Steven R. "Reagan Takes Oath as 40th President; Promises an 'Era of National Renewal' Minutes Later, 52 U.S. Hostages in Iran Fly to Freedom After 444-Day Ordeal," *The New York Times*, January 21, 1981, p. 1.

White, William S. "Seven G.O.P. Senators Decry 'Smear' Tactics of McCarthy," *The New York Times*, June 2, 1950, p. 1, 11.

Wilson, Woodrow. "President Calls for War Declaration, Stronger Navy, New Army of 500,000 Men, Full Co-operation with Germany's Foes," *The New York Times*, April 3, 1917, p. 1.

About the Author

A former president of the South Carolina Historical Association, Dr. Edward Lee is a 36-year veteran of the university classroom, receiving several awards at Winthrop University, where he is a professor of history, for his teaching, including one 20 years ago as a pioneer in distance learning. He is the author of 16 books, which include three on America's Vietnam experience and one on the American Civil War. Frequently, he serves as a media commentator on a wide range of topics. His commentary has appeared on CNN, NBC News, and National Public Radio. For 18 years, Dr. Lee served as mayor of York, South Carolina. Governor Nikki Haley awarded him the State Historic Preservation Award in 2016 for his successful efforts to save the historic York County Courthouse. Currently, he serves as vice chair of the State Archives' Review Board for the National Register of Historic Places.

CPSIA information can be obtained
at www.ICGtesting.com
Printed in the USA
LVHW062043041121
702469LV00001B/7

9 781793 547330